HAUNTED HISTORY: WESTMORELAND COUNTY

by
Ronald L. Murphy, Jr.

ISBN-13: 978-1533065988

ISBN-10: 1533065985

HAUNTED HISTORY: WESTMORELAND COUNTY
by
Ronald L. Murphy, Jr.
© 2016

Other Titles Available by Ronald L. Murphy, Jr.

On Mermaids: An Exploration of Mermaid Folklore from Ancient Origins to Modern Culture

On Dogman: Tracking the Werewolf Through History

Unexplained World of the Chestnut Ridge: A Hike through the Goblin Universe of Western PA

On Wildman: Searching for Bigfoot throughout History

Fiction

The Saga of the Lycans Series

Gypsy Heart - a poetry collection

The Tormented: Ten Tales of Terror

Roland, Dragon Slayer

Find Ronald L. Murphy, Jr on AMAZON.COM for his latest releases

for my Dad

TABLE OF CONTENTS

ACKNOWLEDGMENTS

This book can more correctly be referred to as a volume and not a finished product by any means. I have collected and presented some of the more intriguing tales I have encountered during my research, but in no way have I included every ghost tale that I have been told over the years. I had the plan of presenting a survey of area hauntings as we followed the evolution of human ingenuity in Westmoreland County. Having thus done this, I have regrettably left out some very good yarns that simply did not fit the format that I was following. But I trust, in time, these stories shall also see the light of day in another volume, and those ghosts can rise up out of the shadows and scare you as you flip through the pages of a future book that deals with the haunted happenings throughout Westmoreland County.

I must also point out that I have not included any stories that relate to haunted houses. I must tell you truthfully that I have many cases of hauntings in private homes, but out of respect to the owners of such properties and adhering to confidentiality, I did not include those tales. No one wants people on their property with all manner of evidence collecting gear, stepping through the flowers or stirring up the dogs in their earnest quest to provide evidence of the hereafter. I love haunted houses, but I will not include them in my work in deference to the residential communities in which these structures are situated. Rest assured, we have plenty of other scares without going the haunted house route.

I must also thank everyone that came forward and talked with me as I undertook the daunting task of writing this volume. The Facebook page entitled "Weird Westmoreland" was invaluable to my research and an eager forum for those to tell their encounters with the supernatural. Actually, when I consider it fully, social media was thoroughly helpful as I wrote this book. Thank you all.

I cannot leave out the historians either. Denise Jennings-Doyle and Marna Conrad—thank you for sparking the love of local history in me! Without both of you, these tales would not have been told. I want to thank all the fine men and women of the Blairsville Underground Railroad Museum that bring history to life. I'm flattered to be a member of your fine organization. I am also a member of the Derry Area Historical Society, and this library is stocked with all the information I ever needed to complete this book. They were patient with my questions and were encyclopedic in their knowledge.

I also want to mention how closely I bonded with my family as I wrote this book. Writing is a very lonely endeavor, and much of the time the author lives in a self-imposed exile as the book plugs along. But this book was different. My kids often accompanied me to cemeteries and libraries as I completed this project. My wife, Ashley, was such an asset to me. Thank you. And my father also helped me. Researching with my dad was the best time I ever had with him. Thanks, Dad!

I cannot leave out my editor and publisher at Camonica Books. Dave Cavill is the best friend a guy could have and not only was he efficient, I think you will agree he is one of the best graphic artists in the business. He makes me look much better than I actually am.

Finally, thanks to you, the reader, who yearns, like me, to keep the history of our storied region alive. This is where America was made. We should be proud to call Westmoreland County home. We are in good company with the brave men and women who went before us. These are their stories.

Shall we listen?

RONALD L. MURPHY, JR.

INTRODUCTION

G hosts are the ephemeral impressions from another time. These spirits manifest to us from a particular era or place. These visitations are commonly referred to as "hauntings." When some space is deemed "haunted," we state that the past and present are intersecting and overlapping, creating a paranormal window that allows the observer to witness what was—what used to be. Ghosts are the ethereal reminders of who went before us. These specters are the departed entities of habit, phantoms of routine. They are pages out of an old, dusty book, their visceral stories sometimes all but forgotten, dimmed from view by the relentless passage of time. As you will soon discover, ghosts are capable of blowing away the accumulated cobwebs so we can once more read the pages of that book for ourselves. Ghosts, by their presence, are reminders that the lives lived in the past were of meaning, that they had a purpose and left an important imprint in the world. Ghosts remind us that history matters.

After all, the history of this region is quite old and full of passionate conflict and human turmoil, stretching back before this place was even the United States of America. This area is teeming with tales of bloody aggression and hellish industrial disasters, of legends involving evil curses and chaotic calamity, treachery and insidious murder. It is inevitable that accounts of ghosts would rise up out of these events, haunting the very county in which they were made.

This book will endeavor to uncover and investigate these tales. At this point in our exploration I must impart this important piece of useful information—just because a particular place or space is considered haunted doesn't imply that a supernatural encounter is virtually assured. Indeed, quite a few of the ghosts reported in this book have only been witnessed two or three times over the two hundred (or more) year history of some of these sites. More often than not, when visiting a particular locale with a tradition of a haunted history, one will almost inevitably come back with an educational experience, rather than a paranormal one. Some of these tales of hauntings are rather recent, while others hearken from the very beginning of the French and Indian War. These ghostly subjects inhabit the cemeteries where their memories are interred. They wander as shadows over fields where nearly forgotten battles were waged. These specters are artifacts of the past, images of another time, fleeting tour guides into the monumental history of this county. This book is an attempt to gather these stories and put them into the milieu from which they were formed. You will definitely learn some obscure facts and events that transpired right here in this area of Western Pennsylvania. So keep your eyes opened, but don't expect to see any full-bodied apparitions materialize before you. That said; don't be surprised if they do!

So what are these ghosts? Ghosts are claimed by some to be remnant energies of a life that has not quite passed on, stuck between two planes of existence. Death was an undeniable companion during the formation of Westmoreland County, meted out not only in the battlefields, but encountered daily in the hazardous mines and on the unforgiving railroad tracks. Old World animosities reignited in New World furies. Massacres became a way of life for the immigrants in this county. But all of these events, no matter how unsavory or violent, were the building blocks that fashioned Westmoreland County into what it is today. Through these events, ghostly presences were woven into the fabric of the land.

Most of these ghost tales derive from traditional legends, oft- told stories handed down through the years within families or passed on throughout the isolated homogeny of the small towns that are scattered in pockets throughout the hills and hollows of the countryside. Some of these narratives are centuries old immigrant remembrances while others are much more contemporary. It is in this collision of the past and present that the ghosts dramatically materialize before us. They teach us history more than the state sanctioned plaques that often mark their tangible resting places. As I have implied, ghosts are entities of context, bookmarks to history. And it is through the dead that history seems most alive!

What type of hauntings persists throughout Westmoreland County? Some of these reported ghosts manifest and appear vaporously incorporeal while others are so substantial they cannot be differentiated from the world of the living. At Fort Ligonier, some visitors have even reported taking a picture with a ghost while it posed for the camera! However, this is indeed a rare encounter. More often than not, most ghosts are no more than a psychic impression, a subtle yet profound influence felt by a sensitive soul that results in a very real yet entirely personal experience. This type of ghostly encounter is referred to as an "apparitional experience." But regardless of the way in which a haunting is experienced, ghostly activity can usually be classified into convenient groupings.

Residual hauntings, of course, result most commonly in circumstances involving the sudden loss of life, the energies of the human experience being released into the environment and becoming part of the very landscape itself. These tumultuous events, like frames in a film, are occasionally projected and witnessed as a loop of actions from the past. These kinds of residual hauntings are common in battlefield settings. However, some residual haunts are the result of habituation. Repeated actions, often times quite mundane, embroider into the fabric of a certain area. This kind of residual haunt is sometimes witnessed in the form of an the early 19th century drover that still walks the grounds of the Compass Inn as if it was still a functioning stage stop. Residual hauntings are silent postcards from the past, a moment captured in time, replayed over and over.

Poltergeists hauntings, or hauntings by "noisy ghosts," are also evident throughout this area of Western Pennsylvania. The R and R Station in Mt. Pleasant has well-documented accounts of pots and pans being flung across the room by unseen forces. Poltergeists are the hauntings by unbridled emotions, manifested frequently through tantrums thrown by a tormented soul.

Intelligent hauntings are by those who have died and yet still interact with the living. In the parlance of ghost investigations, an intelligent haunting is also referred to as the "classic" haunting. Many times these specters take the form of the archetypal full body apparitions. It is rather odd, however, but in Westmoreland County, these intelligent hauntings seem to prefer the hallowed confines of churches over graveyards and battlefields. But make no mistake about it; this region has its fair share of intelligent haunts.

The last type of haunting is the demonic manifestation. These nightmarish infestations have indeed been witnessed in the quiet towns of this region. In most of these demonic cases, the evil forces have been summoned to a particular site through the exploitation of a Ouija board or by other conjuring associated with various other misused occultic oracles. Unfortunately, it seems demons are one of the paranormal elements that also haunt certain parts of Western Pennsylvania.

Because of the turbulent history of this county, all of these types of hauntings have been reported in this region. Let us now explore this area more in depth, shall we, and discuss the history behind these hauntings as we travel the highways and back roads of Westmoreland County. These ghost stories beckon to me; the disembodied voices continually wail my name with such lamentable urgency. It seems as if they have something important to show me. Now I will tell you what I have seen and relate the ghostly stories that were told to me as we journey together throughout Haunted Westmoreland County.

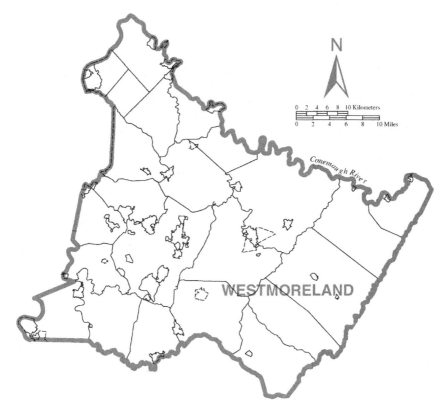

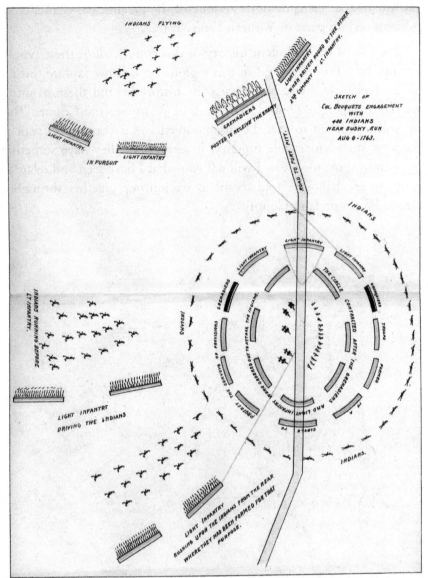

Sketch of Bouquet's Engagements, 1763: Busch, Clarence M, 1896.

To discuss hauntings in Westmoreland County is to talk about a rich history that stretches well back into the 1700s. The most opportune place to begin is before this country was even united. Actually, our starting point will be when this region was fought over by two foreign crowns—the English on one side, the French on the other. The French and Indian War, fought between the years of 1754 to 1763, was the North American theater of the worldwide Seven Years' War. The war was waged between the colonies of British America and New France as well as by Native American allies-- or, more accurately, mercenaries-- fighting for a particular side. Some of the most important battlegrounds in this conflict were fought on the land that would become Westmoreland County.

During this period of heated conflict, forts were constructed in an attempt to establish land rights and keep the enemy at bay. Oddly enough, it seems these very same palisade forts also had the uncanny capability of containing the spirits of those who gave their all in service during this lengthy battle. It is in these forts of the Laurel Highlands that ghosts remind us of this history of a fledgling America.

The battlements surrounding Fort Ligonier

I. FORT LIGONIER

One such military foothold was a British enclave named Fort Ligonier. This installation was utilized as a staging area for the Forbes Expedition, led by the military commander John Forbes, which was an endeavor by the British to wrest control of Fort Duquesne away from the French. Because of its strategic location and logistical importance, this fort along the Loyalhanna River was often under attack. Remarkably, during the eight years of its tenor as a garrison, Fort Ligonier was never taken by an enemy.

Fort Ligonier was constructed in September 1758. By late October,

George Washington had arrived at the place then known as Loyalhanna, an Indian name meaning "middle stream." The aforementioned Forbes renamed Loyalhanna as "Fort Ligonier" after his superior, Sir John Ligonier, commander-in-chief of Great Britain. Almost immediately after its construction, Fort Ligonier suffered the onslaught of various enemy attacks. However, one of the most unfortunate events of the Seven Years War took place less than a month after Washington's arrival, and it may explain several ghosts reportedly haunting the ramparts of the fort in Ligonier and even ranging beyond its walls.

On November 12, 1758, units led by George Washington of the 1st Virginia and Lieutenant Colonel George Mercer of the 2nd Virginia accidentally engaged each other in battle under a blanket of heavy fog and while shrouded by the interminable darkness of the night. In this tragic exchange of friendly fire, two officers and thirty-eight troops were killed or seriously wounded. Could it be that the anguish of this terrible encounter still reverberates in the realization of this accidental massacre, still etched into the land even to this very day? A convenience store directly across the grounds from the Fort Ligonier complex has reported several sightings of ghosts, dressed in full military regalia, rifle in hand and at the ready, creeping through the parking lot in the dead of night. It seems that even after the field were this catastrophe occurred had been leveled with concrete and gas pumps, over two and a half centuries after the events transpired, the terrified emotion lingers and still materializes in the form of those soldiers involved in that infamous night in November.

It is appropriate that Fort Ligonier, with all of its violent events and the outpouring of human emotions, has reported many such ghostly residents. The residual apparitions of soldiers clad in full British military uniforms or the ghostly shapes of American Indians sneaking around the palisades have been witnessed throughout the years. Residual energies have unquestionably imprinted on this site, probably brought about by the constant stress that tormented these troops who were on relentless high alert. Even in death, these steadfast soldiers still follow their orders, keeping continual guard in perpetuity, unfailing in their duties as they stand on their post in an everlasting sentry against the marauding French forces. Indeed, this guarding of the fort was necessary during the hostilities of the French and Indian War. In 1763, Fort Ligonier was attacked twice and besieged by the Native Americans prior to the decisive victory at Bushy Run in August of that year.

This constant state of high alert is witnessed to this day as ghosts have been reportedly seen marching to and fro, hovering eerily over the pointed palisades, before dematerializing into thin air. The underground magazine where the gunpowder was stored has long been the haunt of the spectral artillery keeper, still keeping a protective watch over the fort's supply of gunpowder and ammunition. Many tourists, and not a few workers of the fort, have reportedly witnessed this apparition that is at first believed to be a reenactor. When approached, this military figure simply vanishes!

With the war in the frontier subsequently turning on the side of the British, Fort Ligonier was decommissioned from active service in 1766. Although it was the setting for much strife and bloodshed, the fort held its ground. The site today serves as a reminder of what kind of heroic struggle was necessary to ensure liberty from foreign powers. The residual hauntings evidenced still to this day prove that the fort is yet protected by those serving -- even in the afterlife.

Fort Ligonier Soldier Barracks and Quartermaster Store, Ligonier PA

II. BUSHY RUN

BUSHY RUN BATTLEFIELD

— ♣ —

British and Americans under Col. Henry Bouquet defeated the Indians here, August 5-6, 1763, during the Pontiac War, and lifted the siege of Ft. Pitt.

PENNSYLVANIA HISTORICAL AND MUSEUM COMMISSION

PA State Bushy Run Battlefield Historical Marker

Conflict did indeed spill over into the fields surrounding these forts. Very near the current town of Harrison City, just outside of what would become Jeanette, the Battle of Bushy Run was fought from August 5th to the 6th, in the year 1763, between a British military force under the command of Colonel Henry Bouquet and a combined force of Delaware, Shawnee, Mingo, and Huron warriors. But in that short time in which the conflict waged over the fields, a great many combatants were cut down. This sudden loss of life in such a short time is an essential element in producing hauntings. Bouquet lost 50 of his 400 troops, including seven of the 1/60th Royal Americans, as well as eight civilians and volunteers. Also killed were twenty-nine of the elite 42nd Scottish Highlanders and six of the 77th Highlanders. The ghost of a Scottish Highlander killed in action can be spotted roaming the wood line of Edge Hill to this very day, near the monument that marks the site of the battle that took his life.

Bushy Run Memorial with Bushy Run Battlefield in the background

The ensuing result of this particular clash invoked widespread relief on the frontier since the Indians had been defeated on their own ground. But the Indians, it must be remembered, suffered greatly as well. The confederacy of the Delaware, Shawnee, Mingo, and Huron suffered an unknown number of casualties, which included two prominent Delaware chiefs. A conservative estimate places the total Indian loss of life at about 60 in a period of less than 36 hours. Today, Bushy Run is a solemn field, ensconced by encircling trees, a fitting and reflective memorial to the brave combatants who fought on both sides of this campaign. However, from time to time, shouts of agonized Indian cries disrupt this solitude, the incorporeal laments echoing from within the concealing woods that surround the park, a striking reminder of the fear and pain inflicted by the battle that unfolded so long ago.

After the French and Indian War ended, the King of England, George III, issued the Royal Proclamation of 1763. On October 7, following Great Britain's acquisition of French territory in North America after the end of the French and Indian War, George III declared no settlers where to establish homesteads past a line drawn along the demarcation of the Appalachian Mountains. The problem with this declaration, however, is that subjects of the Crown were indeed still living here; the town now known as Derry just happened to be one of these places. In actuality, generations of white settlers had called this place home. Now, in the light of the King's edict, the people of Derry and elsewhere in the region later known as Westmoreland County were stuck in a veritable no-man's land once it became part of the Indian Territory. Once again, the use of fortified structures was necessary to provide some semblance of protection for a people who were seemingly abandoned by the English Crown. Tensions were high and blood shed inevitable. Very soon after the Proclamation of 1763, defending edifices were raised and the settlers hunkered down for a fight to assert their rights to this region.

(Photo negative due to severe weathering - text reads):Here Rests the Mortal Part of John Peebles. Late Capt'n of Grenadiers 42nd Regiment. Subsquently Major Commandant of the Irvine Volunteers. Born 11th Sept. 1739. Died 7th Dec. 1823. (Aged Eighty Four Years) For Upwards of Forty Years He Served His King and Country with Fidelity and was Severely Wounded at the Battle of Bushy Run in the Warfare (North American Indians in 1763)

*Chief Pontiac in 1763 taking up the war hatchet during the French and
Indian War : Unknown, 19th century*

III. FORT BARR AND FORT WALLACE

The original inhabitants of Westmoreland County were the Monongahela Indians. However, there is a bit of a conundrum involving this
culture. One archeologist stated, "It is in one of our present archaeological
mysteries as to what happened to the Monongahelas. All we know for sure
is that they lived here for centuries, and then about 1600, they disappeared.
To where, we do not know and we do not know the why as well." But psychics have encountered ghostly figures who identify themselves emphatically as Monongahelas, so their spirits are still imbedded within this land.

But an influx of another native culture filled the void left by this mysterious people. According to the insightful documentation of the forts of
this area, compiled in the book Wallace: The Little Fort on the Conemaugh
by local historian Olie F. Merlin, after the French and Indian War, Westmoreland County was, for the most part, under Iroquois control. The Indians that had inhabited this region just prior to the French and Indian War
was the Delaware culture, but they were violently absorbed by the Iroquois.
And it is with the Iroquois that the conflicts of this region collided.

Barr's Fort, a site in New Derry, was erected in 1774. Even then this
area was considered haunted, early accounts from this long ago era re-
marking on the horrible, hellish sounds that came off the Chestnut Ridge,
presumably by menacing, marauding Indians. Fear was a way of life for
those who sought to eke out a living on the frontier. The settlers resided in
crude log homes on the outskirts of the fort, retreating into its protective
confines when the event of an Indian attack loomed. Life was hard and full
of trepidation.

Fort Wallace was another of these early forts constructed in Derry
Township, built along the Conemaugh River at a place then called Broad
Fording. Richard Wallace, a Scottish immigrant, was a farmer in this area.
One of the other first casualties associated with the area of Fort Wallace
did not have to do with waged military action or aggression of any kind.
Indeed, it had to do with a simple visit by Wallace's young sister, Rachel,
who was newly married. She came to Broad Fording to see her loved ones
and as she was attempting to visit her family, she slipped as she stepped
from her boat, falling into the quick rush of the Conemaugh. Her elegant
dress quickly billowed in the rushing water and she was swept away and
drowned within sight of her waiting family. To this day, gossamer light can
be seen from time to time flitting over the waters of the Conemaugh, float-

ing very near the spot where poor Rachel drowned all of those years ago.

But aggression did indeed come to this location and Wallace built his fort between 1769 and 1774. Unlike the stately Fort Ligonier, all of these scattered protective installations, while called forts, were in reality only blockhouses surrounded by a roughly nine foot high palisade of rough-hewn posts. They were temporary defensive structures at best. Therefore, the contingencies of settlers that raised families in the shadows of these forts were dependent upon the other forts in the vicinity for help if the need arose. After all, a fence of wooden posts would not long hold off the hostile intentions of a marauding force eager for blood shed.

In the spring of 1777, Indian hostilities were so intense in this vicinity that many homesteads were abandoned, their owners seeking the safety of the forts. Because of the close proximity, Barr's Fort and the Wallace Fort were dependent on each other. Fort Barr was located on the farm of one of the Barr brothers. Fort Wallace was about five miles distant in the general vicinity of the abandoned town called Cokeville. One particular event tied the Wallace Fort and the Barr Fort forever, releasing ghosts into the environment through the actions that were to transpire in the year 1778.

The Indians generally made their incursions against the outlying forts in the fall of the year. During harvest-time they often became very troublesome, because it was easier to waylay those working out in the open in the fields and to steal freshly harvested supplies. They lurked in the woods, and cut off the unsuspecting settler when he least expected danger. Major James Wilson, one of the earliest settlers to this region, related how he stood in his cabin door, with his rifle in hand, while his wife brought water from the spring. It must be reiterated that the settler's life was one of high alertness and daily stress; fear was a constant companion. All of these emotions are necessary to produce the hauntings reported around these settler sites.

On this particular fateful occasion, the people of Barr's Fort heard the distress shots fired from Wallace Fort; the fort at Broad Fording was under attack! A contingency led by James Wilson raced from Barr's Fort to the aid of those in Wallace Fort. When they reached Wallace Fort, the little party of settlers within the barricade was engaged in heated and ferocious conflict with a large number of Indians. The Indians no sooner perceived Wilson coming to the defense when they proceeded to attack these reinforcements. Wilson had to sound the retreat and attempted to escape the onslaught by making his way to the river. There was formerly a bridge over a ravine that crossed McGee's Run, some 500 yards or so above the site of the fort. Wilson, with a few of his party, had planned to cross this bridge. However, the tactics of the Natives anticipated this retreat and Wilson found the Indians had taken possession of the bridge. Here he was forced to engage in hand-to-hand battle with them. He knocked several of the Indians off the bridge, sending them to their death, thus preparing the way for himself and his friends. He then took his position near a large oak tree on the bank beyond the bridge, and Wilson deftly plied his rifle with deadly effect on his pursuers. But the Indians were too numerous for the little band, and they were compelled to retreat further afield. These settlers kept up a retreating fire all the way back to the scant security of Barr's Fort.

Alas, only about a mile out from Wallace's Fort, the first of the Barr brothers were killed. When they had nearly reached the Barr's Fort, Robert Barr was killed. As it was, Robert was engaged with several Indians, fighting hand-to-hand. Major Wilson shot one of the Indians, who fell dead on Barr. The next instant a tomahawk was buried in Barr's skull. This was the way of life and death on the frontier.

The day ended with a retreat into the safety of Barr Fort, the toll on Indian life barely accounted for. The Indians were buried were they lay, scattered throughout the woods and fields between the forts of Wallace and Barr. To this day, ghostly Indians are seen around the former sites of Barr and Wallace Forts. So too, are transparent children, dressed in Colonial clothing, seen playing amongst the trees that grow along the banks of the Conemaugh River. These young spirits are haunting reminders that very young lives were consumed in the conflict for the possession of this territory. But all of these ghostly figures are vacuous testaments to the nearly forgotten history of the forts that were constructed after the end of the French and Indian War.

The last recorded attack on Fort Wallace was actually after the signing of the Peace Treaty of 1783. An Indian wearing a uniform indicating he was in the service of the English approached the fort waving a flag of truce. The settlers, fearing deception, shot the man dead, burying him where he fell. Perhaps this man simply wanted peace, weary from all the years of fighting. Perhaps the ghost of this man still haunts this now wooded area, seeking the peace he sought.

To this day, disembodied moans are heard and foggy figures seen around the area of Fort Barr, which is now called New Derry, and in the general vicinity of the once bustling coal-mining town of Atlantic. It is indeed quite probable that residual forces still remain from the sudden deaths resulting from mining accidents common to this town, coupled with the energies connected to the killings of frontiersmen and Indians that yet linger. All of these forces seem to be generating a kind of perfect paranormal storm that produces so many supernatural sightings in this area of Westmoreland County.

IV. Fort Palmer

Fort Palmer was a very important Revolutionary fort located on the very edge of Westmoreland County, not far from the winding Conemaugh River. It was strategically situated to the north of Forbes Road. The exact date of its construction is unknown, but we do know there was a land transfer on March 11, 1771 between Robert Knox and John Palmer. By the year 1787, the maps of the area showed a Fort Palmer, so it can be assumed the fort was built while Palmer owned it the property, somewhere between 1771 and 1776. This fort remained among one of the last utilized of the forts erected by the settlers as a defense against the Indians.

Like the other forts throughout the county, Fort Palmer was also a protective stockade blockhouse. It was depended on many times during the Revolution, sheltering the farmers from the Indians fighting on behalf of the Crown. In one letter written during this period, it was stated that the settlers were so harassed by outside forces that they had to continuously live within the confines of the fort, unable to work in their fields due to constant threats by the Indians. Here the farmers and waylaid travelers remained while danger was imminent. When the attacks gradually ceased and threats seemed to dissipate, the settlers went forth from the fort with their families, venturing back to their homesteads or continuing on their perilous travels. In fact, Fort Palmer was so essential to the settlers of the frontier during this pivotal time in history that it was mentioned in the journal kept at Fort Ligonier.

But the safety provided by Fort Palmer was not without its casualties. This was a time of total war, with every person on the frontier a target. Reports from this time indicate that eleven men were killed and scalped near the fort. But it is the children seen running through the woods to this very day, witnessed as vaporous specters near the former site of the fort, which is so haunting. Where the fort once stood there stands now a golf course, and it is on this course that the apparitions have been witnessed throughout the

years. In October 22, 1776, two children were killed by the marauding Indians within two hundred yards of the fort, unwary victims of the war that
waged around them. When seen, these phantom children seem to be playing, chasing each other in blissful games, still untarnished by the horrors
of the war that shaped America. Perhaps these woods were happy places to
them, and even now, they return periodically to continue their game that
they were mercilessness taken from all those years ago.

V. FORT ELDER

A couple miles outside of Murrysville, just off a road that intersects
with the hustle of Route 22, Fort Elder stands as a silent sentinel. It
was built by a settler named Robert Elder in an area that would come to be
known as Richland Farm. This small blockhouse was erected in 1783 as a
safeguard against Indian incursions that came from across the Conemaugh
River. This little fort is unique in that within its confines it held a spring-
house that would enable the settlers to hold out for a longer duration in the
event of a siege by the natives. But it is not the events of war that haunt this
site. Indeed, the ghosts often seen prowling about the lands surrounding
site of this fort are the spirits of Indians, seemingly filled with despair.

Sensitive witnesses describe these shimmering Native American
ghosts as 'filling the observer with instant despair.' Unfortunately, in his
quest to settle the frontier, Robert Elder built his rather obscure little fort
on the site of a sacred Indian graveyard. The Indians weep over the intru-
sion into the realm of their hallowed ancestors, their intended eternal rest
forever disrupted by white settlers uprooting the trees and turning the soil
to grow crops. Indeed, many feel that the Indian attacks on Fort Elder were
not so much as a hostile offensive affront but rather a vain attempt to drive
intruders off the land of their dearly interred forefathers.

VI. HANNASTOWN

The quest for liberty seems to transcend even the grave. This is the reason, then, why a little place known as Hannastown still reports apparitions haunting its grounds. However, the British did not calculate the lingering effects of the French and Indian War and its aftermath. This war had indelibly left its mark on the American colonies. A scent of nationalism was in the air as settlers stood their ground in direct opposition to what they deemed as foreign edicts. The price of the war was painfully expensive for the British and the logistics of controlling the newly forfeited French territories was difficult and ultimately impossible. The British therefore looked to the colonies to help pay the costs of Empire building. These excessive taxation levies was the impetus that lit the fuse that ignited the powder keg of the Revolution. It was through this fervor that Independence began to take shape, taking hold first in a little settlement called Hanna's Town.

Hanna's Town in 1770s: Homer F. Blair, 1941.

This frontier village was founded in 1773 as the seat of the newly created Westmoreland County, and known at the time as "Hanna's Town". The town actually grew around the tavern owned by Robert Hanna, who set it up to aid travelers along the Forbes Road, the main route into the Ohio Country from eastern Pennsylvania. This tavern also served as Westmoreland County's first courthouse. This settlement, now called Hannastown, was settled primarily by Irish and Scotch-Irish, though the surrounding area was mostly the farmsteads of the Pennsylvania Dutch. Little Hanna's Town was active in various issues associated with the Revolutionary War. The residents, forced to defend themselves without any military aid from Great Britain, felt as though the British Crown had abandoned them. Without aid, they were even more disgruntled at having to pay taxes without any benefits. In this little corner of Westmoreland County, the Hanna's Town Resolves were written and signed in May of 1775. The Resolves were a unanimous proclamation claiming that freedom from Great Britain should be the primary concern for the people of the colonies and that Hanna's Town would form themselves into a unified militia to defend the Western borders of the Colony. This document is one of the most direct challenges to British authority preceding the Declaration of Independence. Before most other colonial communities took a stand, Westmoreland County residents proclaimed their willingness to take drastic measures to maintain and defend their rights against British oppression. To punctuate this truth, they illustrated this fact in the creation of their own flag.

Standard of the 1st Battalion Westmoreland County PA aka "Proctor's Flag." Created as a direct result of Hanna's Town Resolves. Only surviving colonial era "rattlesnake design" flag. Gold paint on red cloth: unknown designer from Hanna's Town, 1775.

The field of this flag was blood red. The red on white cross represents that of the English cross of St. George, the white on blue cross is the representation of the St. Andrew's cross. The British symbolization on the flag was meant to boldly indicate that those who resided in Westmoreland County were ready to resist foreign tyranny. In the center of the flag is the iconic rattlesnake, coiled and ready to strike, keenly focusing on the symbol of the British Empire. The snake's 13 rattles represents the original colonies. The lettering reads "DON'T TREAD UPON ME," a motto adopted as an anthem for American freedom. Rebellion was in the air.

DONT TREAD ON ME

Traditional Gadsden Flag "Don't Tread on Me": Christopher Gadsden, 1775.

Hanna's Town was also an important center for the recruitment of militia for the western campaigns against the British in Detroit and their Native Americans allies. In an attempt to crush the relief forces mustered in this little yet troublesome town and in one of the final battles of the Revolutionary War, Hanna's Town was attacked and burned on July 13, 1782 by a raiding party of Indians and their British allies. The town never recovered, and in 1786, the county seat was moved to Greensburg, which was then called Newtown. The village of Hanna's Town was eventually rebuilt, but after Forbes Road was rerouted through Greensburg, the settlement stagnated, and eventually most of it became farmland.

The events that occurred in Hanna's Town were the catalyst by which America was to take shape. And occasionally a ghost can be seen still parading in vaporous uniform to remind us that real men and women played not only an important role in winning our freedoms, but some gave everything they had to assure this. Now this historic site consists of the reconstructed Hanna Tavern/Courthouse and three vintage late 18th century log houses, a reconstructed Revolutionary era fort and blockhouse, and a wagon shed. Of course, several Colonial ghosts also haunt this place.

Employees here have heard 'strange' noises, and some have reported objects moving without any human assistance. Paranormal investigators have heard raps in intelligent response to their questions. There are claims of people seeing a figure in a window of the tavern. And some people even report seeing an older man in period clothing walking between buildings and even talking to them, only to disappear before their eyes. But the ghost most often seen is one of a young girl, seemingly lost in the fields that surround the fort that stood guard over this site.

It is presumed that this ghost girl is the spirit of Margaret Shaw, a brave 16 year old, who left the confines of the fort to rescue a young child playing idly in the fields as the marauding Loyalist forces swept in to burn the town. Margaret was shot in this act of bravery and she died a short time later. Her ghost is a fitting reminder that innocence is the first casualty of war.

Historic Hannastown Sign

Reconstruction of Hanna's Tavern (the original courthouse and jail)

Hanna's Town 2nd Tavern and Jail Reconstruction with Pillory

Historic Hannastown Old Fort Walls

Hanna's Town Historical Plaque

Hauntings along the Highways

I. Inns and Houses of the Stage Coach Routes

To overcome the Appalachian barrier in colonial days, traders drove trains of packhorses up and down the mountain ridges, with each animal bearing a typical load of some two hundred pounds. Even though the Indian trails had been widened to accommodate wagons, the cost of transporting goods over such formidable terrain prohibited commerce on any extended scale. This cost was lessened by transitioning from Indian paths before the French and Indian War to military roads after the Revolutionary War.

After the conflicts that afflicted Westmoreland County had dissipated and British rule transitioned over to self-government, the roads used as military supply lines were now used to link towns and states in the mostly peaceful enterprises of commerce. Many military highways became stagecoach thoroughfares, following the most direct routes.

It was over these ways that this county expanded in commerce and in hauntings.

The Forbes Road was a historic military roadway in what was then

British America, constructed in 1758 from Carlisle, Pennsylvania, to the confluence of the Allegheny and Monongahela rivers in what is now downtown Pittsburgh. This road was 300 miles long and named for Brigadier General John Forbes, the commander of the 1758 British expedition that built the road during the French and Indian War in Pennsylvania. The Forbes Road and Braddock's Road were the two main land routes created by the British which cut west through the Appalachian frontier. These roads were essential for troop movement during the French and Indian War. Amazingly, these routes are still utilized to this very day. Present day U.S. Route 22 mostly follows portions of the Forbes Road from Monroeville through a town now named Forbes Road and through Hannastown to Latrobe. The Lincoln Highway, which, in this region, is mainly the present highway named U.S. Route 30, largely followed the Forbes Road between Latrobe and Bedford. Still later, a portion of the Pennsylvania Turnpike (Interstate 76) largely followed a portion of the Forbes Road from Bedford over the Appalachian Mountains to Carlisle. Many historical markers indicate locations along the original route where Forbes traveled with his army. At the extreme westerly edge of Westmoreland County, a Forbes Road marker is located along US 22, 1.2 miles east of Murrysville.

Historical Marker of Old Forbes Road near Ligonier as in 1758.

The Braddock Road was a military road built in 1755. No more than a twelve-foot wide footpath, it was the first road to cross the natural obstacle of the consecutive ridgelines of the Appalachian Mountains. It was constructed by troops of the Virginia militia and British regulars under the leadership of General Edward Braddock, and it did indeed open new territories for settlement.

The Northern Turnpike was a road that passed through Murrysville, where a tollhouse built in 1788 still stands, a restored reminder of the importance of this route. Carl Patty, president of the Murrysville Historical Society, states that Pittsburgh was the gateway to the West. As it happens now, tolls were paid as a cost for the privilege to travel along the pike. The fees paid were used for the upkeep of the road. These enabled goods to be transported much safer and quickly over this route, allowing trade to flourish along this way.

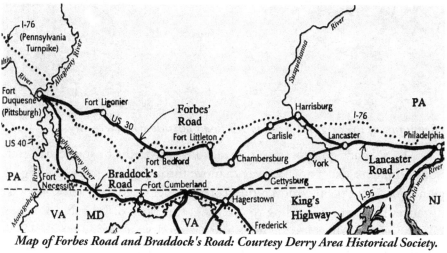

Map of Forbes Road and Braddock's Road: Courtesy Derry Area Historical Society.

Remnants of the original Braddock's Road outside Fort Necessity

These roads quickly transitioned from foot-traffic to stagecoach traffic as people needed a quicker way to move through the ever-expanding region. Not only a people-mover, the coach also delivered mail across the vast distances it served. According to the insightful work of John N. Boucher, "Wagoning, as a business between the east and west, began about 1818, and reached its highest point about 1840, or perhaps a year or so earlier." But the stage was by no means without its risks. Travel was hard and often arduous. In fact, elderly passengers on the coach or those with a serious ailment, often packed a furnished "death trunk," a box outfitted with burial clothing and money to pay for an undertaker as well as instructions on how to contact the family of the deceased. It was not rare that someone setting out on a brief excursion was never seen again! After all, the trip to Pittsburgh was known to take as long as three days under certain conditions. So the specter of death loomed over the wagons that made their way along the stage route.

Let us now travel the Forbes Road and visit two of the haunted inns that once served the weary travelers and drovers who depended upon the stagecoach.

THE COMPASS INN

The Compass Inn is an historic inn and tavern located in Laughlintown, Ligonier Township, Westmoreland County. It is a 2 1/2-story, five bay log and stone building in a vernacular Georgian style, built in 1799. It was restored in 1970, and operated as a local history museum. The property even includes a rebuilt barn and a restored blacksmith shop.

Two ghosts have been seen in and around this historic site. The first is the apparition of a drover, the ghostly image of the man responsible for leading a group of animals as they made the arduous journey along the stagecoach trail that would become Rt. 30. One of the employees at the Compass Inn first thought the full-bodied apparition was one of the many historical reenactors that frequent the grounds. However, the sighting took place at night, a strange time for a reenactor to be working long after the museum had closed. The employee called out to the figure who stood still at the edge of the inn. As she approached to investigate the figure further, the drover simply…vanished!

The other ghostly inhabitant of the inn haunts the kitchen area inside the stagecoach stop. It is a small body, his appearance seemingly corporeal. He hides under the kitchen table or peeks out from under the chairs. He appears frequently to children that are brought to the inn during school field trips. Many of the former owners of the inn did indeed raise children here, but no death of a boy seemingly eight to ten years old was ever documented. It seems this spirit found peace in this place, and prefers to visit this plane of existence from time to time simply to interact with those he would consider compatible playmates.

The Compass Inn, Laughlintown, PA.

WASHINGTON FURNACE INN

Just up Rt. 30 from the Compass Inn is another tavern and boarding house. This cut-stone edifice was constructed by Johnson, McClurg and Company. The Washington Furnace Inn was built very near to a cold blast charcoal furnace in 1809. The inn was short-lived, eventually abandoned in 1826. In 1848, the inn along the highway was restored by John Bell and Company and was in operation until 1854. It served hungry and thirsty travelers as well as providing rooms for a night's stay. But like many other historic sites, it again eventually fell into decay and sat forgotten once again along the now busy Rt. 30.

However, in 2012, two local businessmen purchased the property, breathing new life into the historic edifice. It seems that the reconstruction of this property also resuscitated the ghosts who lingered in the cobwebs and shadows of the vacant inn. The sound of footsteps can now be heard as unseen occupants make the rounds of the inn. Unusual cold spots are reported as guests eat at the bar or use the restroom. And there have been the reports of misty fogs in the shape of full-bodied apparitions that lurk the halls and dark recesses of the building. It seems that these stops along the old Forbes road had such amiable amenities that some patrons simply refuse to leave.

The Washington Furnace Inn: photographer unknown, 1930s.

Moving onward from the Forbes Road, we now detour to another colonial route created by a different general. This route, known as the Braddock Road, passed through the western end of the future town of Mount Pleasant in 1755, opening this wilderness of Westmoreland County to settlement. With the subsequent colonization and inevitable expansion came the need for transportation to link this town with the rest of the state and beyond. And as we have seen, with the road also came the necessity of providing travelers with places to stay. Very soon, the business of the inn along the highway was a lucrative venture.

THE R AND R STATION

The year of Mount Pleasant's first non-Indian resident is unknown, although one source states that at the time of the American Revolutionary War, there was a settlement of "not more than a half dozen houses." This area of scattered farmsteads was to have a population boom with the advent of the turnpike. One of the inns that boarded workers and travelers became the R and R Station.

This inn was built in 1882, and it apparently has some customers that checked in more than 100 years ago and remain there to this very day. Originally known as the East End Hotel, the purpose of the edifice was to house the workers building the turnpike. After the completion of the project, the inn would then take in travelers needing a night's lodging. However, the building that would be come to be known as the R and R Station had another use then–simply providing rest and sustenance to road-weary wayfarers.

During the winter months, the ground was too frozen to dig graves. So the bodies of the deceased would need to be stored somewhere until the spring thaw to be properly interred. This is where the R and R Station came into play. The basement of the inn served as the winter morgue, housing the bodies of those unfortunate enough to die during the dead of winter. In time a bar was put in down in the basement. Until quite recently, bartenders behind this basement bar have reported not only unexplained noises, but also have attested to witnessing black shadows walking back and forth throughout the bar area.

But this whole building seems to be filled with spirits. In fact, one ghost investigation team has reported making contact with over twenty ghosts! The most mischievous ones are of a little boy and girl. Often these ghosts have been identified as poltergeists because of items being thrown or doors opening and closing. But many psychics insist these ghosts are intelligent hauntings playing with the living. Believed to be the children of a worker that labored on the turnpike, these children have been seen to manifest on the third floor. But most of the time their presence is made known by the sound of little feet running up and down halls. Many guests have opened their door to see what the commotion was about only to look at a vacant hall. Also, the boy spirit has the knack of bouncing balls as if he would like to play. The little girl, when seen, is described as being dressed in a white gown. She has been reported as venturing down to the first floor, curiously peeking around corners.

However, these are not the only ghosts of children haunting this inn. And the next haunting is a sad tale. On the third floor, the ghost of a pre-pubescent girl is said to haunt the room in which her father, a former own-er of the inn, confined her. Fearing she was mentally ill, the father shunned her from society. One psychic feels as if the young girl was simply dealing with the stress of adolescence and the father, and older man and a widower, felt this incarceration was for the best. Indeed, it wasn't, and the young lady committed suicide, her spirit still locked within the room.

On the second floor is the ghost of known as the Victorian Lady. She has been seen sitting in a chair at the end of the long hallway. She wears the dark colors of mourning, traditional to this time period. Sometimes she is seen as a full-bodied apparition, other times she is witnessed only by looking into a mirror that hangs in the hall across from the chair in which she sits. There her reflection is seen, weeping in an unknown sadness that consumes her long after she has passed from this world.

On the third floor, many guests have told of the smell of burning cigars. According to investigators, this is the evidence of the presence of a mob boss, who enjoyed a fine stogie. According to legend, this mobster hid out at the quaint, inconspicuous inn. But his anonymity was not to conceal his whereabouts, and he was killed at the R and R Station.

R&R Station Restaurant as seen today.

The most recent member of this ghostly cavalcade seems to be that of a milkman, who died in the R and R in 1936. He was delivering milk on the terribly blustery day of January 23, when the trolley derailed from the accumulation of ice and careened into the R and R Station, killing the milkman and many other unfortunate souls. Incidentally, the trolley connected Mt. Pleasant with the town of Morewood, another haunted locale that we shall visit a little later.

So why is it that the R and R Station seems to be so supernaturally active? Well, some investigators claim that the inn is also the site of a vortex, a portal that allows the spirit realm to come and go into this plane of existence. In fact, a few researchers have pinpointed the exact location of this portal—room 15, on the third floor, in the bathroom. So if you ever venture to the R and R Station and find yourself on the third floor in room 15, maybe it is best if you don't flush!

OLD CONGRUITY INN

Our next stop takes us to an inn just outside New Alexandria. The Congruity Tavern was built right around the year 1820 by the Kirkpatrick family and stands along the historic Northern Turnpike, which would later become U.S. Route 22. The 2-1/2 storey stone house with brick end chimneys was a tavern for many years, but records indicate that after 1881 it was most certainly transformed into a private residence. And it is at this juncture of the Inn's history that now forms the basis of its haunting.

The Congruity Stagecoach Inn

Newlyweds by the name of Maggie Buchanan and Robert Stewart purchased this property with the intention of creating their lives under its roof. In fact, lovingly written copies of several old love letters from Robert to his young wife Maggie still exist, preserved in a pocket flap of an old silk pillow at the house. It seems so much love was centered in this house that Maggie herself is still around. All hauntings are not frightening encounters with specters whose earthly lives were miserable and wretched. Indeed, the majority of hauntings involve an area that held a deep connection for someone, a connection so powerful it transcends even life itself. Maggie is a gently protective spirit, looking after her home like a doting 19th century woman. She has been heard whistling a gentle, lilting tune. Sometimes the sound of clattering china is overheard, as if she is still keeping up with the dishes. Clothes have been reported to be discovered folded and put away before the owner even removed from the dryer. Maggie is a domestic ghost, a caring spirit of her hearth. The love she felt in this place was obviously like heaven on earth.

II. CANALS

Rivers are capable of facilitating paranormal activity, according to claims. It may be the raw power of the natural, kinetic force that enables ghosts to materialize; or it may be, like the tape in a recorder, events simply imprint in the rushing waters. Ghosts seem attracted to rivers, as if they depended upon them. Whatever the case, the Conemaugh River, the meandering feature that demarks the edges of Westmoreland County, has been the scene of hauntings throughout the years. The Pennsylvania Canal that carried cargo near the former site of Bairdstown, Westmoreland County, provides us with one worth mentioning

In 1826, the state legislature authorized the first segment of the Western Division of the Pennsylvania Canal. This canal was constructed within the Kiskiminetas-Conemaugh river basin. This basin flows through a picturesque mountainous terrain that forms the very heart of the historic coal-producing areas of this region of western Pennsylvania. The canal linked towns together in a way that the stagecoach could not. Now the river towns of Westmoreland County could reach Pittsburgh in a mere twenty-four hours. The voyage, although not without peril, was far safer and much more comfortable than the constant jostling promised by travel in wagons over the stagecoach route. River voyages tended to be much smoother, the canal boats being pulled, as they were, by ropes attached to mules that were led purposefully as they walked the towpaths built along the banks of the Conemaugh. With the popularity of the canal, towns located along its route soon prospered.

Bairdstown was one such town. Now it no longer exists, save for a few foundations, haunting reminders of lives that used to call this area home. It has been reclaimed by the woods and the thick brambled undergrowth. The town is now lost to history, a mere footnote in the chapter on canal operations. But a ghost reminds us that Bairdstown played its part in shaping Westmoreland County into what it is today. A faintly glowing blue mist is seen from time to time, forming under a murky deep water section of the Conemaugh, then gradually rising up out of the slow flow of the river, lingering for a moment over the water, and then leisurely wafting onto the western shore, creeping up the bank, then spilling through the trees, before coagulating into the vaporous form of a young man. Who is this man?

Coal Barge Pulled up Canal by Mules, 1904: Frank Hill.

His name has been lost to time. Perhaps he was an immigrant who worked the canal yard in Bairdstown at the advent of the canal system; this scenario is likely, as immigrant towns lined both shores of the Conemaugh. What is known for sure is that a young man working on a barge at the advent of the canal system took a tragic step and fell off the barge into the depths of the turning pool, known as "the ferry hole." The ferry hole was a deep area of the river that was dredged out so that barges would be able to turn within the confinement of the river. Into the depths of these waters he submerged, never to be seen again. Many believe this spectral fog is the spirit of the young man, finally able to break the surface of the river, where he makes his way once again to the safety of the river bank, a residual haunting reminding us that even the unknown life played a part in this County's transformation.

It must be noted that this area of the Conemaugh River is less than a mile away from Broad Fording, the site of the drowning of Rachael Wallace, whose apparition appears as a very similar mist over the waters of the river.

HAER No. PA-82-1

A typical coal canal with mule-drawn barges.
Delaware & Hudson Co. Canal Coal Pocket, Wayne, PA

III. Railroads

L ike rivers, railroads seem to be a conduit for paranormal phenomena. It is as if all the human energies exerted into the creation of the rail system, and the kinetic power for the trains themselves, is stored in a similar way as a charge is stored within a battery. Very many hauntings in this region seem to tap into this latent energy in the rail lines in order to manifest as ghostly figures.

In 1846, the Pennsylvania Railroad was chartered from Harrisburg to Pittsburgh. The West Penn Railroad, now known as the Conemaugh Division of the Pennsylvania Railroad, was built in 1861 and has been in continuous operation ever since. The railroad was much more efficient than the canal, and soon supplanted its use. This fact is illustrated in the area of the Packsaddle Gorge of the Chestnut Ridge, where the rail line was laid over the pilings and edifices of the canal system itself.

Overgrown railroad bridge abutment in near Cokeville.

Indeed, Westmoreland County is abundantly supplied with railroads. Nearly one sixth of the Pennsylvania line between Pittsburgh and Philadelphia lies within its bounds. In fact, the Pennsylvania Railroad was the first railroad across this county, built in the early days of railroad engineering, and this rail line has been a prominent factor in the development of our industries throughout the region and beyond.

It must be remembered that this creation of the rail system took an exorbitant amount of manpower to bring it to fruition and countless deaths are directly linked to the railroad that runs through Westmoreland County. Many of these deaths were of the immigrant, brought to America for the sole reason of constructing the railroad. As the demand for laborers increased, railroad company solicitors were sent by to Europe to procure workers. Many of these workers came from Ireland. The job of the company solicitor was made all the easier in Ireland because in the mid-19th century, the Emerald Isle was in the suffocating grip of the potato famine.

Irish Railroad Workers, B&O Railroad: photographer unknown, 1850-59.

This terrible blight reigned from 1845 to 1852. It is sometimes referred to, mostly outside Ireland, as the Irish Potato Famine because about two-fifths of the population was solely reliant on this cheap crop for a number of historical reasons. During the famine, approximately 1 million people died and a million more emigrated from Ireland, causing the island's population to fall by between 20% and 25%. Whole villages were brought over and housed in barns set up on farms throughout Westmoreland County. Sometimes towns that had been in disputes with other towns over nationalistic ideals or religious concerns-- mainly hostility between the Protestant and Catholics-- were housed together in what soon became a veritable powder-keg of potential violence. On occasion, this resulted in an explosion of pent-up rage that costs many immigrant lives.

PACKSADDLE DISPUTE

In the summer of 1850, a fierce clash occurred in the Pack Saddle Valley between two factions among the Irish labor engaged in the grading of the Pennsylvania Rail Road through this gap. The canal had previously cut through this pass, but with the advent of the railroad and the efficiency and expediency of the travel and the relative safety, the tracks were laid over the canal works. The two gangs were known as the Far-ups and the Far-downs or the Leicester-men and the Munster-men. Rifles and other weapons were used; several men were killed and many more were wounded. Father Pollard, a priest from Greensburg, attempted to quell the violence, but to no avail. It is along these tracks that men have been seen working, sometimes witnessed in broad daylight. Yet witnesses report that the clothes in which these men are dressed are from a different era, and the tools they work with are antiquated. When approached they have been known to move off into the trees, never to be seen again, or, more frequently, they simply disappear!

Packsaddle Gap as it looked in 1891: Photographer unknown.

GANG WARFARE IN MILLWOOD

In 1852, as the Pennsylvania Railroad continued its sprawl throughout Westmoreland County, another infamous dispute by workers boiled over into murder. A force of Irish workers, in a fever of hostility stemming from their strained relations back in their emerald homeland, settled their Old World dispute in the New World. The incitement of this battle dated back to at least the era of the Battle of the Boyne, which occurred in 1690. The issue was the unresolved tensions between the Catholic and the Protestants. This conflict was to be seen again in the little town of Millwood.

About 200 Irish immigrants, known as Far-downs, who were laboring on the Packsaddle and Bolivar section of the rail line, came to Millwood on a Sunday in June to do battle with 300 Leicester men, who were employed one the rail line from Hillside to Greensburg. The term Far-downer first appeared in America as early as the 1830s and referred to immigrants from Ireland who came to work on the canals and railways. In effect, it was used to describe manual laborers. Far-downer has an even deeper embedded meaning. The word seems to have been applied only to the Irish who were Catholic. Far-downer was never used to define a Protestant. The expression of Far-downer derives for the Gaelic tongue and the words "fear donn," which means "the dark man." The connotation between these Irish workers and the image of the enslaved Southern black should not be lost in translation. The Irish, even long after the Civil War legally ended slavery, were still classified in the same ethnic grouping as the black man. Both were seen as inferior humans. Indeed, in a letter written in July of 1902, a railroad correspondence seeking labor plainly states "We want mainly good Italians, [Poles], and Hungarians. We do not want colored help, or Irish, under any circumstances." Imagine the working conditions a half century before the enlightened 20th century! This racism meant that Irish workers would naturally align themselves with local friends and kin, staying close with those who journeyed over with them.

They met in Millwood in such a heated mêlée that the townspeople who looked on armed themselves in self-protection for fear that the violence would spill over to the adjacent houses. Many members of the Irish gangs knocked the handles off their pick axes with the intention of using them as shillelaghs, while the others in the factions had various guns at their disposal. When they did indeed square off, two men were killed instantly and twenty-three were severely wounded. The dead men were buried where they fell, and several of the wounded eventually succumbed to their injuries. When additional tracks were laid, a decade or so later, the graves of these fallen men were covered by the rails.

A one-time resident of Derry states when she was a high school student, nearly a decade ago, she and her friends where walking the railroad tracks one night. Too young to drive, the tracks were an easy way to walk from one friend's house to another. The tracks were a useful and familiar pathway, level and straight, although a very dangerous route and now a completely illegal way to traverse. As the group ambled idly along the risers, laughing and joking like typical bored teens who live in small towns, they noticed the night became somewhat darker. "It seemed as if we were walking into another world," the witness recollected. Walking these tracks as you leave town, one becomes cut off from seeing the road and houses by trees that form a barrier on either side. "It became difficult to breathe, like we were all having a panic attack." As it happened, the group was now in the very area of the fight between the two Irish factions. As the feeling of dread filled them, one of the girls in the group began to cry. "We felt like running, but it had become so dark we couldn't see anything." They needed help.

The help came in the form of a man dressed in black, carrying an oil-fueled lantern in his hand. This form of a person seemed to appear out of the very night, his flickering flame burning away at the interminable blackness. He did not say a word but beckoned the teenagers to follow with a motion of his gloved hand. "We were speechless. But if we didn't follow him we knew something very bad would happen," the witness recalled. The figure led them away from the tracks and to a partially hidden trail that cut the dense brush and up through the woods that circled through the trees and lead back to the town. Eagerly they hurried to the trailhead. As they turned to thank this stranger, instantly the man with the lantern vanished before them. Filled with a curious combination of fear and gratefulness, the teens raced home, believing they had seen an apparition from another time.

Surveying the wreckage of the 1912 Ligonier Valley Railroad Accident: photographer unknown, 1912.

SHADOW PEOPLE OF THE DERRY TRACKS

The little town of Derry is ideally suited for major railroad facilities because of its ready access to water from McGee Run (essential in the era of steam locomotives) and because it sits atop a slight summit along the railroad right-of-way. In Derry's heyday in the late 1800s, it had four hotels, mainly to provide for the needs of railroad workers, as well as a massive roundhouse for locomotive maintenance and an immense railroad yard. Derry served as the terminal for Pittsburgh commuter trains until 1964, when the Pennsylvania Railroad ceased operating its commuter service. The annual Railroad Days Festival serves to remind residents of Derry's railroading heritage.

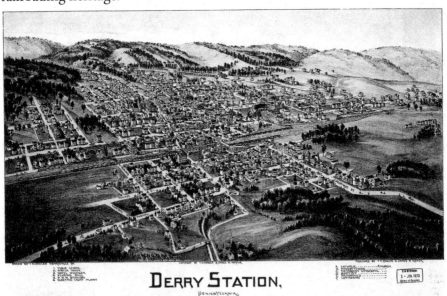

Derry Station in 1900, Aerial View: Illustration Fowler.

Little else remains of Derry's railroading boom. Most businesses have long left the vacant main street, and Derry has been reduced to a residential town. But make no doubt about it, this fading town is the haunt of shadowy figures, the presumed victims of the tragedies on the tracks that still trouble this sleepy little town. The very rails may provide the energy fueling some of the paranormal activity.

The first deaths reported on the train tracks that pass through Derry date back to September of 1895. Two young men were crushed to death under a train. A couple years later, in 1897, two people were thrown from their horse-drawn buggy when the horse was spooked while crossing a bridge over the tracks. Then in 1907, a brakeman fell from a train to his death. This is just to name a few of the more unusual accidents associated with the first decades of the train's impact on Derry. This is not including derailments and various other tragic mishaps that, if written, would be a book unto itself. Suffice it to say, the tracks making their way through Derry have taken a toll on the lives of many since they were first laid down. And it does indeed seem ghosts are attached to these tracks for that same reason. Black figures are witnessed crossing the tracks or walking directly into oncoming locomotives.

When the streetlights come on as the sun goes down, these spirits begin wandering the tracks. Sometimes no more than mere shadows flashing in the corner of the eye, this shadow people remind us that these railroad tracks have exacted a deadly toll, costing many their very lives.

By not respecting the sheer power and brute force of the trains and the inherent deadliness of the railways, careless trespassers on the tracks have met their demise throughout Westmoreland County. Some of these deaths have resulted in hauntings. Here is one in which ghosts have recently been observed.

DEAD MAN'S CURVE

The community of Youngwood was established in 1899 and was built on land owned by a certain John Y. Woods, a farmer in the area. In creating the name Youngwood, John Y. Woods took his own family name and combined it with his maternal grandfather's name, which was Young. Youngwood owes its existence to the Southwest Branch of the Pennsylvania Railroad, which ran from Greensburg south to Uniontown and Fairchance. In 1900, a large classification yard was built for sorting railroad cars, and this railroad yard provided Youngwood's economic base for many decades.

Dead Man's Curve was supposedly named for a dead hobo. Some years later at the same spot, a gruesome suicide by train may have reinforced this nickname. Railroad tracks are dangerous places, and whatever the origin, the ghost that haunts Dead Man's curve illustrates this fact. The specter seen along these tracks is a victim of circumstance, his earthly existence ended amid steel rails and the sparks of a braking train.

While the railroad tracks appear to have ghostly apparitions haunting its winding way throughout Westmoreland County, a few railway tunnels seem to hold spirits within their bleak confines. Like a haunted house, these tunnels are said to echo with moans of the deceased and are alleged to be the habitation of the spirits of the dead. The first we shall visit is called, appropriately enough, the Witch's Tunnel. In this tunnel, the denizen is said to be that of a vengeful witch's ghost.

WITCH'S TUNNEL

Paranormally speaking, some researchers view tunnels as a conduit, a tangible portal to another time and another place. While the witch may be a legend, something is seen in this area. Apparently, the apparition slips in and out of this reality, using the tunnel to carry its energy in the same way the tracks carried locomotives. It is possible that a spirit uses the Witch's Tunnel because the rock in which it is constructed and the stored energy associated with the tracks allow the spirit to manifest as an apparition.

Just outside of Greensburg is an 825-foot tunnel known as Carr's Tunnel. However, over the years, it has come to be referred to as "the Witch's Tunnel." It was originally built in 1856 for the Pennsylvania Railroad. The railway line it was associated with, now dismantled, once ran from Donohoe Station to the now-vanished Carney Station, near the Carney coalmine, and on to Latrobe. So why the association with the tunnel being haunted by a witch? Well, many people assume it must be cursed due to the events that unfolded in 1907.

In 1907, three fatal accidents occurred at Carney Mine. The first accident was on January 21st, when a Russian immigrant was crushed in a cave-in within the mine. On July 29th, an Austrian miner was killed by a fall of slate. Then on Dec. 12, an Italian miner was likewise crushed to death. All of these occurrences seem to have been too coincidental for the miners and townspeople to accept, so of course witchcraft was blamed. Remember, this was a town of immigrants who brought Old World folk-beliefs with them.

One legend states that a particular unnamed woman was accused of the curse ad summarily hanged within the tunnel, far from the eyes of those who would not understand this form of Old World justice. Many subscribers to this tradition feel that the witch that cursed the mine now resides in the tunnel built to carry the coal from that mine. It seems as if this witch is doomed for eternity to the dark isolation of the mine. The same mine that took those lives in 1907.

DEAD MAN'S TUNNEL

Very near to Lynch Field in Greensburg, there is yet another tunnel reportedly home to paranormal activity. Thus, tunnel only became necessary after the construction of the Southwest Branch in the 1870s. It enabled westbound traffic to cut under the railroad and join the Southwest Branch without interfering with eastbound traffic. Tunnels like this were called a duckunder. The tunnel is now known as "Dead Man's Tunnel" because of a death that occurred on the tracks that pass through. It has been reported that several homeless people inhabited the tunnel. After a night of excessive imbibing, the unfortunate souls passed out along the tracks and were run over by the train that was passing through the duckunder. Witnesses report that the spirits of these individuals still dwell within the darkness of the tunnel, hiding from prying eyes, not realizing a train had killed them.

Not only do the tracks and its tunnels seem to be haunted by those who lost their lives in the effort to lay them across the county, but so too do the train stations that serve them. Let us now explore two of the ghosts said to haunt the train stations along the rail lines.

GREENSBURG TRAIN STATION

This grand station is located at 101 Ehalt Street, on the corner of Harrison Avenue, in the city of Greensburg. It was designed by architect William Cookman for the Pennsylvania Railroad in a style known as Jacobean Revival. The Pennsylvania Railroad began servicing Greensburg in 1852, at the very dawn of the railroad era, and a temporary structure was utilized as the town's station for several years. However, in the early 1900s, the railroad was expanded from two tracks to four tracks, and the tracks were elevated to create a more nearly level right-of-way for locomotives. These changes necessitated a new station, which is the current station that we see today. When it opened in 1911, four active tracks passed by the station, and there were two passenger platforms, one platform serving two eastbound tracks and one platform serving two westbound tracks. The station is on a level below the tracks, so that passengers would walk through a pedestrian tunnel and then up stairs to one of the two platforms. These pedestrian tunnels are the location of the classic apparitions reported. It was here that a local woman named Jayne Ferguson witnessed an intelligent apparition nearly four decades ago.

In the late 1970s, Ms. Ferguson was waiting on the passenger platform for a train bound for New Jersey so she could spend the summer with family. By this time, rail travel was declining and the Greensburg station was relegated to a flag stop. A flag-stop is when the intended passenger must physically flag the train to stop by waving their arms. It was 5am and rather foggy, so Ms. Ferguson recalls that she was desperate to board that train.

The Greensburg Railroad Station as seen today.

Just as the sun began to break through the fog, Ms. Ferguson recalls seeing a nun making her way off the platform across the tracks from where she stood and down the pedestrian walkway. She could see clearly that this nun wore the old style habit and she readily recalls the impression that the figure was from a different time. Ms. Ferguson looked at her mother, who agreed that she too saw the figure. It was a seemingly solid person, moving purposefully down the stairs. But suddenly the nun stopped and looked at the mother and daughter. Their eyes locked, seemingly discerning each other. And then the nun simply vanished. "She just disappeared," swears Ms. Ferguson. "I am a Methodist, but at that moment I thought about saying a Hail Mary!" Maybe this ghost was departing from a train that dropped her off many years ago, retracing her steps as she made her way to Seton Hill University, which sits on a hill not far from the train station.

Currently, there are only two tracks passing through the station, each served by a separate platform. The grand building is now owned by the Westmoreland Cultural Trust.

THE LATROBE TRAIN STATION

The town of Latrobe was built out of the railroad boom. In 1852, Oliver Barnes, a civil engineer for the Pennsylvania Railroad, laid out the plans for the community that was incorporated in 1854 as the Borough of Latrobe. Barnes named the town for his best friend and college classmate, Benjamin Latrobe, who was a civil engineer for the B&O Railroad. His father, Benjamin Henry Latrobe, was also a man who was a pivotal figure in architectural history; you see, he was the architect who rebuilt the United States Capitol in Washington, D.C. after the British set fire to it during the War of 1812.

Latrobe PA Railroad Station as seen today.

Thus, Latrobe's location along the route of the Pennsylvania Railroad helped Latrobe develop into a significant industrial hub. The railroad, of course, needed a station to serve its passengers, and the station was opened in 1903 by the Pennsylvania Railroad as part of a project to elevate the right-of-way as it passed through Latrobe. The architect, William H. Brown, used an eclectic Late Victorian style in the brick, one-story station. The station was listed on the National Register of Historic Places in 1986. This historic station exists, but currently it has been repurposed, serving as an upscale restaurant. Due to the small number of rail passengers, Latrobe

Station is now reduced to a flag-stop. This station has suffered the fate of most of the stops in Westmoreland County. There is no longer a ticket office available at the small shelter, just a little row of utilitarian bench seats, which serves as the current station. This current state of the stop is nothing like the former grandeur of the once elegant Latrobe station. But apparently, the ghost of a former station attendant does not realize that the grand Victorian station is no longer sheltering passengers. An elderly man, wearing period dress appropriate to the turn of the twentieth century, has been seen in the restaurant, checking the time on a silver pocket watch, as if the train was still the preferred method of transportation. This ghost appears to be a residual reminder of the time when the station bustled with rail passengers, eager to make their train. And maybe that is the best way to remember the railway industry–not as a declining method of transportation, but as a once opulent way to travel when tracks connected this country and linked us all together like a patchwork quilt.

Quarry Accident in Derry, 1913

THE GHOSTS OF LABOR AND INDUSTRY

I. THE QUARRYMEN

As Westmoreland County moved from being a series of scattered frontier villages, it slowly established itself as an industrial center, relying on the land's natural resources for its raw materials. In the year 1906, a sand crushing plant of the Derry Glass and Sand Company was located at the southeast end of the town of Derry, just beyond the town limits, on the small stream called McGee Run, which has, as its source a spring on the side of the Chestnut Ridge. A steam powered stone crusher operated on South Ligonier St., where it pulverized the sandstone to make sand. This sand was then sent to the glass factory in Derry and on into Jeanette, where it was used in the prosperous glass industry located in that city.

The sandstone quarry, known as the Booth/Flynn Quarry after its owners, was located on the northwest side of Chestnut Ridge, on the north fork of this stream, about one and one-fourth miles above the mill. It is connected with the plant by a tram road. The quarry is about 465 feet above the mill in elevation, so that the cars can be let down by gravity. A hoisting engine has to be used, however, to assist in returning the empty cars. Five loaded cars are let down at one time, while five empty cars are being hoisted. There was an accident during February of 1913 when seven men were killed and nine others injured seriously, when a rope holding a train of cars on an incline at the Derry works of the American Window Glass company parted and the cars rolled off the track.

A carload of workers were traveling down the tramline after work and were celebrating the end of the working day a little early, drinking whisky and smoking cigars, when the tramline broke sending them on a terrifying ride down the tramline to their deaths. The first car jumped from the track and was followed by the other cars and their human freight. The train and the men were piled in an agonizing mass, some bodies strewn over the rocks and through the trees, the others spilling into the waters of McGee Run. The accident happened suddenly. So suddenly, in fact, that some of the men who died in the event still don't realize that they are dead!

Erie researcher Patricia Coleman, a medium and a 30-year veteran of paranormal investigations, examined the site of the tram derailment. For years, people have reported shadowy black figures walking through the trees, or the shapes of men flashing in the corner of the eye. Ms. Coleman, however, can communicate with spirits, and has the gift of visibly seeing these ghosts. On the Ridge, without knowing anything concerning the tragic accidents of the tramcars, Ms. Coleman saw several of the deceased quarry men wondering around aimlessly at the exact site of their death. Some of these apparitions were residual, but some, too, were intelligent hauntings, the ghosts of young men confused about what had happened or too concerned with their past responsibilities to simply let go. But on this lonely spot on the Chestnut Ridge, several miners who died tragically one their way home from work over a century ago still have not passed from the site of the stone quarry in which they worked.

II. GLASS MAKING

Much of the quarried material taken from the Chestnut Ridge was hauled by railroad to the glass making factories in Jeannette. First incorporated as a borough on June 7, 1889, Jeannette earned the nickname as "the glass city" in recognition of the numerous glass plants founded in the area, with those factories contributing to the city's original stature as the first large manufacturing town in Westmoreland County. In fact, the impact of the glass industry was so significant that the city's name actually comes from Jeannette E. Hartupee McKee, the wife of H. Sellers McKee, a local industrialist who cofounded the Chambers and McKee Glass Works.

Historically, there were as many as seven significant glass factories operating in the city of Jeannette. These factories included some of the most well known in the history of the glass industry in America. These plants supplied the country with everything from plate glass windows, to bottles, to milk glass, and much more for many decades. Some astonishing estimates indicate that Jeannette once produced somewhere between 70-85% of the world's glass! Unfortunately, Jeannette's glass manufacturing was one of the early United States industrial victims, falling to the foreign competition that made it less expensive to produce glass overseas.

Westmoreland Glass Company Furnace 1: Jet Lowe, c. 1950.

While glass production was in full swing, one of the most well-known factories was the Westmoreland Glass Company, founded in 1889. This factory produced fine glassware and was the pride of the Jeanette community. Apparently, that pride exists even beyond the grave. Although no deaths were recorded at this site, ghosts linger here nonetheless, continuing their trade even from beyond the grave.

The artisans at this factory crafted fine examples of different types of glass. The Westmorland Glass Company's main color was milk glass. Milk glass is an opaque milky white or colored glass. It can either be blown or pressed and comes in blue, pink, yellow, brown, black, aside from the color white where it gets its name. From the 1920s to the 1950s, it was estimated that 90 percent of the production was milk glass. Collectors still seek this glass, considering it a valued piece of Americana.

The Westmorland Glass Company also produced carnival glass in the 1920s. Carnival glass is molded or pressed glass, always with a pattern and always with a shiny, metallic, 'iridescent' surface shimmer. This carnival glass was reissued as novelties and as pattern glass in carnival treatments in the 1970s until the plant closed in 1984. The company also produced high quality hand-decorated and cut glass.

Smells of sulphur are reported issuing forth from the vacant and decaying factories, as if the skilled artisans still work within the bowels of the plant. Disembodied voices are heard echoing through the steel frames as if a foreman is calling out orders to workmen. Black shapes have been seen still moving about the abandoned plant, their shadowy presence even turning on motion sensor lights in adjacent houses.

Remants of the Westmoreland Glass Company Furnace 1 as seen today. Fire has gutted most of the long-abandoned structure.

In the tiny village of Grapeville, a patch town that is almost rotted away, the old Westmoreland Glass Company factory defiantly stands. Even in death, former workers still are punching their times cards. Black shapes have been seen in a foggy procession, filing out of the factory at quitting time. The ghosts remind those who witness them that there was once a thriving industry in this town.

Maybe this is what haunts the residents more than otherworldly specters.

III. COAL MINING

The mining of coal has been an active industry in Pennsylvania's bituminous coalfields since the late-1700s. Towards the last half of the nineteenth century, the demand for steel generated by the explosive growth of the railroad industry began to further impact bituminous coal production in western Pennsylvania. The early room-and-pillar mines relied on manual labor to cut the coal at the working face and then the mined coal was hauled from the mine by horse and wagon. Later the coal was unloaded onto trains to fuel the insatiable furnaces of the steel mills.

Miners at American Radiator Mine, Mount Pleasant, 1936.

There were so many coalmines operating in Westmoreland County for so many years, it is difficult to ascertain an exact number of fatalities. As it was, many of the laborers, from other countries, didn't speak the language. Their employers probably didn't even bother to learn the names of the miners who worked the coal seams. Sometimes deaths were noted by nationality and no name was assigned to the body. Many of these miners died in dark underground tunnels utterly alone, missing their loved ones who waited for them a world away. That was the life of an immigrant coalminer. But the coalmines were a source of income, and the mines needed workers. These energies that emanated from the miners who lost their lives remain, consequently resulting in a residual haunting of apparitions imprinted on a specific area. The energy may be stored in the rock of the landscape and released due to natural earth pressures. Or this life force may be energy stored in an underground water source as well. Whatever the means of these hauntings, many patch towns throughout Westmoreland County are haunted by those who went underground and never returned alive.

DARR MINE DISASTER

Mines were dangerous places to work. Cave-ins were a constant fear, workers tormented by the knowledge that at any moment the seam they worked could give away and come crashing down on them. Also, natural gases could easily be ignited by the flame of the miner's headlamps. This indeed seems to be the cause of the Darr Mine Disaster.

On December 19, 1907, an explosion in the Darr Mines, located in Rostraver, claimed the lives of 239 miners. Only two survived. The cause was supposedly the open helmet lamps of the miners setting off a gas pocket in a section of the mine, although this excuse was probably perpetuated to spare the Pittsburgh Coal Company owners from responsibility. Locals claim ghosts haunt both the mass gravesite where the unfortunate miners are interred, and also reside in the still open shafts of the mine. Male voices are reportedly heard arguing in the wee hours of the night, although no one can make out the words. As most of the miners killed in the blast were Hungarian, it may be the witnesses are hearing the ghosts of those immigrants. Smoky images in the shapes of the figure of a person, charred and smoldering, have been seen. These graphic spirits are the horrific reminders of the horrors of this event. One visitor, unaware of the Darr Mine disaster, heard disembodied voices whisper "Oh God." This witness may have heard a desperate prayer from beyond the grave. You see, the Darr Mine event could have been much worse if it were not for two hundred Orthodox miners skipping work to celebrate mass on St. Nicholas Day.

Miner with redesigned headlamp, Mount Pleasant, 1936.

Coal Miners Descending into Hazleton Mine: 1905.

PA Miners prep for dynomite blasting: Sheldon Dick, 1938.

Miner trapped in cave-in debris: c. 1909.

NORVELT COKE OVENS

O riginally called "Westmoreland Homesteads," Norvelt was established on April 13, 1934, by the federal government as part of a New Deal homestead project. With 250 model homes, Norvelt provided housing, work, and a community environment to unemployed workers and their families during the Great Depression. This planned community was a progressive departure from the dismal patch towns usually associated with towns owned by the coal companies. This community was eventually renamed "Norvelt" in 1937 in honor of First Lady Eleanor Roosevelt and her interest in the project.

Norvelt was meant to improve the quality of life for laid off workers. However, as the working conditions in the mines hardened people, Norvelt became a rough and tumble town. Bituminous coal miners and operators often fought one another during the nineteenth century. Miners developed a reputation for militancy, increasingly going on strike and joining unions to fight for better pay, shorter hours, and safer working conditions. Norvelt, you see, was home to miners that worked for the HC Frick Coal & Coke Company, putting it squarely in the middle of the USW management clashes of the 1930s.

Ghosts of miners are reportedly seen walking in the woods, and sounds of rocks being tossed in a pond have been heard. But it seems as if these intelligent hauntings are a bit confused, thinking people walking in this area are members of the company police?

Ruins of Fort Palmer belgian ovens for coke production.

The Coal and Iron Police was a notoriously brutal conglomeration of men owned by the coal companies who exacted harsh judgment on the mining towns that they served. As this country tried to regain its footing in the second half of the 19th century, states enacted laws giving many business corporations the authority to create their own private police forces or to contract with established police agencies to establish a semblance of order. The Coal and Iron Police of Pennsylvania was a company police force that later became notorious for its anti-labor vigilantism. The Coal and Iron police came into being right after the Civil War and lasted until 1931. Often common gunmen, criminals, and adventurers were hired to fill these commissions and they served their own interests by causing the violence and terror that gave them authority. Many worker disputes we met with a violent response from the Coal and Iron Police, and quite a few deaths were blamed on these forces.

The Pennsylvania State Police was created as an opposing force against these renegade law enforcement groups. However, the State Police were little better than the corrupt Coal and Iron Police at its inception. They could be bought off by wealthy mine owners, and they often looked away at various affronts against humanity. Sometimes frustration dealing with the immigrant workers became so stressful for members of the State Police that they would ride roughshod through shantytowns, killing anyone getting in their way. And this meant men, women and children. The town of Atlantic witnessed such a massacre by the State Police, who killed several members of an immigrant mining encampment.

THE MOREWOOD MASSACRE

The massacre at Morewood involved the production of coke. Coke is a fuel with few impurities and high carbon content and, in the case of Westmoreland County; the coke was made from coal. This fueled various industries, such as in the production of glass. Glass manufacturing was a foundation of the local economy in Mount Pleasant, with Bryce Brothers commencing operations in 1850, and L. E. Smith Glass in 1907. The invention of the Bessemer process of steelmaking in 1859, which required coke as fuel, had a dramatic impact on the region. The town prospered as coal deposits were mined and from which coke was subsequently made. However, the lives of coal miners in the outlying "patch towns," which were company-owned mining towns, were arduous, and labor-management disputes became frequent. The strike in Morewood, west of Mount Pleasant borough, was the most violent of the area's strikes.

The Morewood massacre was an armed labor-union conflict. On April 3, 1891, nine coal miners were shot and killed during a strike that called for higher wages and sought an eight-hour workday. Deputized members of the 10th regiment of the National Guard fired two rounds into the crowd, killing six strikers outright and fatally wounding three more.

A Pennsylvania state historical marker describing the event was erected in 2000 at the Route 119 overpass on Route 981 (Morewood Road). It is very near this marker that strange and unexplained shimmering shapes are still witnessed in this area. Are these the ghostly specters of miners killed for striking simply for better pay and a regular workday? To this day, Mount Pleasant is referred to as "Hell Town." It is this pivotal event that gave this town that moniker. And their spirits remind us of the horrors endured that led to the working conditions we have today.

Not only were the company policies Draconian, the very law enforcement organizations of this period were frequently not playing by the rules if palms were greased properly. Into this void of lawlessness, crime syndicates quickly sprang up, wanting a piece of the fortune made in the mines. One particularly ruthless society reigned in the coal towns throughout Pennsylvania. In Westmoreland County, this group was active in Torrance, Brenizer, Latrobe, and Greensburg. However, the mining town of Pandora was hit the hardest. Now no more than farmland, with no trace of the mining industry evident, Pandora and the neighboring town of Atlantic were bustling mining centers with the owners amassing riches never imagined outside of being a railroad magnate. It was easy pickings for the opportunistic members of the Black Hand.

THE SCOURGE OF THE BLACK HAND

Don't go down that hollow," parents would warn their children. "People get killed down there." This was an admonishment meted out to many children by parents who were warned by their parents. In a sleepy little town like New Derry, what could possibly be all the fuss? This memory passed down from one generation to another was indeed on of the most terrifying yet nearly completely forgotten histories of Westmoreland County.

New Derry was founded in 1815 and was, like many other small villages, an essential hub in the commerce of the area, especially in mining and in coke production. Many people worked in this area, in the mines of Pandora and Atlantic, Superior and Red Shaft. The labor conditions were dismal and arduous. Often times a man would go off to work and never return home. Death was a fact of life for the mostly immigrant workforce. A living wage was barely given to the men who toiled away, their faces black from the bituminous dust of these mines and their lungs choking with the smoke of the coke ovens. If working conditions did not get them, many workers would be waylaid by the Coal and Iron Police and be intimidated into paying bribes or protection money. Lawlessness was the law of the land. Quite a few of the landowners and company administrators did indeed become wealthy in this business. And here begins the story of the Black Hand.

Symbols of the Black Hand, 1904.

*Joseph Boomer
Greensburg Police Chief
from 1888-1920s: c. 1900.
Newspaper reports list
several shootouts involving
Chief Boomer, his deputies,
and Black Hand members
while attempting arrests.*

The Black Hand was a type of extortion racket, not a criminal organization as such, though the Mafia did indeed practice the Black Hand's established terroristic techniques. The Black Hand garnered its name from the practice of shaking someone's hand and subtly depositing a slip of paper that had a black mark written on it. This warning meant that you had been targeted. Later, the Black Hand would add fanciful decorations such as daggers melodramatically dripping blood, revolvers spitting fire and bullets, crudely drawn skulls and crossbones and the inevitable sketch of a human hand. The roots of the Black Hand can be traced back to Italy to as early as the 1750s. However, the term as normally used in English specifically refers to the organization established by Italian immigrants in the United States during the 1880s who, though fluent in their Southern Italian regional dialects, had no access to Standard Italian or even a grammar school education. A minority of these ostracized immigrants formed loosely organized criminal syndicates. By 1900, Black Hand operations were firmly established in quite a few of the Italian-American mining communities, such as those in and around New Derry. The personal touch of a handshake soon became less intimate and a more anonymous letter would be sent to the potential victim in which bodily harm, kidnapping, arson, or murder was outlined as well as the demands that would negate such actions. The letter demanded a specified amount of money to be delivered to a specific place. It was decorated with threatening symbols like a smoking gun, hangman's noose, skull, or a knife dripping with blood or piercing a human heart, and was in many instances, signed with a hand, "held up in the universal gesture of warning", imprinted or drawn in thick black ink. According to the author and historian Mike Dash, "it was this last feature that inspired a journalist writing for The New York Herald to refer to the communications as "Black Hand" letters—a name that stuck, and indeed, soon became synonymous with [this society]." Thus, the term "Black Hand" was readily adopted by the American press and morphed into the idea of an underground, yet well-organized, criminal conspiracy that came to be known as "The Black Hand Society"

Murder was definitely a vital part of the Black Hand's modus operandi. Reports of bloodied bodies lying in the streets of New Derry, their throats cut, became terrifyingly commonplace. An area known as the Hollow, which the present day Route 982 now roughly follows from New Derry to Bradenville, was the dumping point of many murdered bodies left as a warning that the Black Hand meant deadly serious business. Ghosts continue to be seen as shadows in backyards around this area. It is believed that the ghosts of these murdered victims are the specters often witnessed crossing this route in the dead of night, apparitions appearing in the headlights of oncoming cars as emaciated corpses with no eyes, the sockets deep black pits.

Members of the Black Hand after arrest in nearby Fairmont, WV: c. 1903-1910.

One of the most devastating attacks committed by the Black Hand in Westmoreland County occurred in the coal mining areas involving the towns of Superior, Atlantic, and New Derry in 1914. Six deaths resulted from a planted dynamite charge, the subsequent explosion and the resulting fire killing the innocent victims in horrendous violence.

This terrible event occurred in the early morning hours in an area known as "The Barrens." The exploding dynamite immediately claimed four lives and inflicted injuries on nearly 25 other people, collateral damage in an extortion plot not paid, destroying thousands of dollars' worth of property. It was eerily similar to the Bradenville explosion that had happened earlier that same year.

The target of this terrorist attack was the home of a Mr. Noah Panizzi, a wealthy merchant. His innocent, sleeping children paid the extortion demands -- with their lives. Three boys, brothers, one 17, one 10 and the other a little fourteen month-old baby, were burned to death, only charred fragments of their bodies being found, recovered in the aftermath from the smoldering shrapnel. The force of the explosion reached as far as to Latrobe, while the big blast was felt as far away as Greensburg and Blairsville. Windows within a radius of two miles of Superior were broken and plaster was knocked from walls five miles away all in an attempt to extort something as fleeting as money.

Why are places like this area of Westmoreland County haunted? The answer is quite simple-- because of events like this! Young lives, full of expectation, immediately cut-off in a violent terrorist attack, are the impetus of many of the apparitions. So there is little wonder why ghostly cries are heard in the night, or the flickering will 'o wisps are seen like fire dancing in the trees. Memories of events like this are seared into the very fabric of this region.

IV. The Steel Mill at Monessen

The industry of steel is the pinnacle of the labor industry in Westmoreland County, reigning well into the 20th century. The mills relied on the miners to provide the coal that fueled their furnaces and the railroad to transport the raw materials that were created within its crucible. The principal raw materials for an integrated mill are iron ore, limestone, and coal (or coke). And Westmoreland County was rich in these resources.

The steel-mill towns of Pennsylvania helped give birth to the modern urban society. Mill towns flourished from the mid-1930s through the mid-1970s owing to the strong steel unionism achieved during like the coal-mining town of Norvelt Franklin Roosevelt's New Deal and the plentiful steel profits in subsequent decades. To many Americans, steel-mill towns were drab and gritty, suffocating in smoke, and peopled by "foreigners." Even the great "steel city" of Pittsburgh was not really a metropolitan center like Chicago or New York, but a set of mill towns strung along its riverbanks. Beneath the smoke, however, one could find diversity and dynamism.

The steel towns changed decisively with the arrival of immigrants from southern and eastern Europe in the 1880s. And it is in this group of immigrants, within the factory's heat and in molten steel in which the legend of Joe Macarac was conceived.

As the story goes, Joe was a sort of patron saint for steel workers. He was a Croatian steel worker who, in some accounts, was killed by falling into the liquid steel. After death, he was a forged steel ghost that haunted the mills, saving the lives of those workers who took the same perilous misstep that cost him his life. Many steel workers reported hearing of someone saved by the ghostly Joe Macarac, the phantom reaching out a ghostly arm and pulling a man to safety in the midst of his free-fall to certain death.

Aeriel View of Monessen, Pittsburgh Steel Company
Blast Furnace & Coke Plant: Jet Lowe, c. late 1950s.

Joe Macarac may haunt the steel mill in Monessen. However, in 1928, the Croatian ghost was unfortunately absent.

Monessen is the most southwestern municipality of Westmoreland County, and steel making was a prominent industry in Monessen. In a practice that is shocking by today's standards, and by no means limited to only the mills in Monessen, pay was determined by ethnic background. Not only was there a discrepancy in the inherent racism of the wage system, a typical workweek was 84 hours! Workers were required to work 7 days a week at a shift of 12 hours. Coupled with the heat and exhaustion of working in the mills, one can easily see how fatal errors were made.

In 1928, an accident occurred and the ghost of the unfortunate soul was still seen walking within the mill until quite recently. An employee of the American Sheet and Tin Plate plant met with a horrid death while at work on a Saturday morning. The man reported for work as usual at 7 o'clock to clean the boilers. The man used an electric lamp attached to a long cord and used a compressed air cleaner to clean the boiler. Unfortunately, this unfortunate soul perspired freely while at work in the confined heat of the boiler and he was electrocuted by the conductivity of the power cord and his sweaty clothes. He was burned fatally on his upper torso, charring him almost unrecognizable. It is this spirit, this burnt steel worker, who is seen prowling about the mill, 75 years after his death, a hideous reminder that the industry that created so much could also destroy in one agonizing moment.

Today, many old steel mills sprawl across the landscape of Westmoreland County and beyond, into the Ohio River Valley, forming an area designated as the Rust Belt. This once proud mills that poured molten steel around the clock now stand idle, decaying into rusted skeletons, haunting the towns that once depended on them for their survival. These mills are the tangible ghosts of an industry that has died. The eerie moans of the wind through its decimated ribs can be heard, reminding us of the history that now rots away. Sometime, as you drive past one of these crumbling monoliths, stop for a moment and ponder what this phantom apparition is trying to tell you. It is a tale about a shared history, a story no longer told but one that should never be forgotten.

Abandoned Lehigh Specialty Melting Co.

Lost Loves

The emotion of love can bind people together throughout their lives. It also seems, in these next three tales, love also extends to beyond the grave. Here in Westmoreland County, several ghosts still seek those they lost while in earthly form. Witnesses to the phantoms on spectral quest to find the one the love is not so much terrifying as it is hauntingly sad and evocative, touching the heart and soul with the sympathy of a lingering loss that nothing can replace.

Mount Pleasant Aeriel Drawing: Fowler, 1900.

Very near the town of Mount Pleasant, deep in the woods that grow to the edge of the concrete sidewalks and parking lots, there is a small valley that is seldom visited due to the remote location and rugged terrain. The hollow of this valley is known as Moccasin Hollow, and the name stretches back to before the French and Indian War. Much of this tale is, of course, legend, but the ghosts witnessed by those who have stumbled upon them know some of this legend is indeed true.

THE MAIDEN AND THE HUNTER

The tale unfolds thusly: once the Indian warriors of the Laurel High-lands were called upon to assist in an attack instigated by white set-tlers. On their victorious return they carried back a spoil of war— a small child with dark eyes and hair and a ruddy complexion. What certainly is not legend, but historic fact, is that many white children were indeed taken from settler families after a battle. There are many reasons why this may have occurred. It was a common practice throughout this area to cap-ture and adopt people from enemy tribes, particularly children, teenagers, and women. In fact, one of the great Underground Railroad conductors in Western Pennsylvania, John Graff, who lived for a time in Unity Township, related how the natives kidnapped his mother, Barbara Baum, when she was nine years old.

The one overriding explanation to why kidnappings occurred may have been to introduce new genes into a community that had a dwindling diversity. In this tale of the kidnapped settler boy, this situation seems to be the reason for the abduction. However, once the child was introduced into the tribe, assimilation was often a smooth transition. In fact, mistreating someone once he or she had been adopted into a tribe was considered evil and many Indian legends and folktales revolve around some villain who abuses an adoptee and is punished for this misdeed. Adoptees usually also had full social mobility, and often wound up in leadership positions or married to an important person in their new tribe. The young abducted boy was adopted into the wigwam family unit as one of the braves and soon was so indoctrinated into the culture of the Native American that the youth lost most any recollection of life with his own people. He was given the Indian name of Hodenosauni, which is roughly translated, appropri-ately enough, as "captured in a log cabin." As the boy grew within this new culture and in the woodland environment, he developed a strong physique and because of his already dark complexion, he was soon assimilated into the ways of the Iroquois. His prowess as an athlete soon manifested, and his ability as an archer was unparalleled in his tribe. But he also had some remnants of his environmental learning from his family within him and he proved himself quite adept with mechanical reasoning and artistic creativi-ty. He soon became a proficient maker of splendid bows and arrows.

There was a certain custom within this specific tribal society that whenever an Iroquois maiden disclosed a desire to make her own home and obtain a mate for herself, a festival of archers would be held and a contest in archery would be conducted so that the best hunter and thus the best provider might make the perfect husband. As this tale goes, soon after Hodenosauni had reached adulthood, he had become a hunter and marksman of legendary renown. It so happened that the daughter of the chief wished for Hodenosauni for herself. The young man also loved her with all of his heart. The maiden was quite astute in the art of moccasin making, having been trained by a famous craftswoman of the village. So the chief's daughter set out on making her beloved a gift of finely crafted moccasins to wear to the event wherein Indian maidens would choose their mate. To assure not only Hodenosauni's love but to make certain he was the victor in the contest for her hand in marriage, the chief's daughter went to the medicine man. The medicine man told her the charm that would work would be to sew a pocket on the tongue of the moccasins she created and place in that pocket a little ball of beeswax with which Hodenosauni might prime his bowstring before he competed in the contest. This being done, the Great Spirit would guide the arrow to its mark.

The maiden informed Hodenosauni of the charm, and the young man was a bit skeptical about the medicine's man advice. However, he gave into to the plea of the beautiful girl and decided to at least put this charm to the test. He had spent many hours honing his bow for the competition and feathering the arrows that were to be used at the festival. Hodensauni had worn his new moccasins and had been successful in the hunt on every adventure into the forests.

The day of the festival arrived. In the morning was held a hunting competition, in the afternoon would be the marksmanship event, and in the early evening there was the wedding ceremony. Hodensauni went into the competition fully aware of his skills, and not a little convinced in the magic of the medicine man. At the outset of the competition, Hodensauni knelt in the forest to get a little of the wax to prime his bow. As he did, he aroused a white-tail deer from its bed. The young man quickly nocked his arrow, drew, and deftly felled the doe with an expert shot. He was crowned the victor of the morning event.

The marksman event was held in the afternoon in a field serving as a range. Most of the young Indian men were preoccupied with the girls, decked in their finery, who watched and giggled as they gathered around the field. But not Hodensauni. He was focused on his one true love and the task at hand. Using the charmed wax, he was able to outshoot the other young Iroquois men and was named victor of the archery event.

That evening, so the story goes, Hodensauni took the chief's daughter as his wife. They lived happily for many years, he becoming an even greater hunter as he matured, his wife a doting and loving wife. But their story was too soon interrupted by the white men pushing into the Iroquois territory and building military garrisons. Inevitably, the first shots of the French and Indian War were fired and Hodensauni and his wife were the only survivors of an attack on their village. Seeing that their way of life was over and to preserve the lives of he and his wife, Hodensauni decided that assimilation back to the world from which he came from was necessary. He sold his pelts and hides from his hunting and trapping endeavors and as his interaction with the white man continued, the language of his youth gradually returned. So he was giving advice on farming and animal husbandry. He earned enough to purchase a few cows and even left the woods behind and created for he and his wife a farmstead, even building a log cabin in the fashion of the settlers. Hodensauni even changed his Indian name to an English one, taking on the surname of Hunter. He became a part of the church, and at his death, he was even granted a Christian burial. But this would simply not do. The man who became Hunter was laid to rest between to rocks deep in the woods, and on his feet were placed the moccasins with their magical charm still intact.

But, as the legend goes, many a night, deep in the woods of a place that is to this very day referred to as Moccasin Hollow, two ghosts can be seen, shimmering full body apparitions moving knowingly through the trees. It is said the ghost of Hunter and his wife meet on certain nights of the year, the charm of the medicine man transcending even death. It is in these phantom hugs that their transcendent love is once again complete; however, they refuse to cross-over to the other side because they long only for each other's embrace on those few nights of the year when they can again meet.

THE PACKSADDLE GAP GHOST

The Packsaddle ghost knows too well that the power of love has an energy that can survive even the ravages of death itself. But this specter of a mountain hermit continues his haunting as a form of penance, for it was by an accident committed from his carelessness that his true love was tragically taken from him.

Near the northwestern corner of Westmoreland County, the Conemaugh River used to run swift and white, its waters stirred into deadly cataracts that caused many a loss of life as river travel was attempted through this gorge. Before white settlers ventured into this region, the Packsaddle Gap served as an Indian path. However, the Pennsylvania Canal construction tamed these swift waters around 1832. The canal was used until the late 1850s, the progress of the locomotive replacing the slower and much more dangerous way to travel.

This is the story of a ghost of a mountain man named Tom Skelton, who lived as a veritable hermit in the mountainous area of the Packsaddle Gap, long before even the canal was proposed. He was an untamed hunter, illiterate and uncultured, who fell madly in love with the daughter of a frontier settler. Her name was Maria, and the beautiful Maria loved Tom as well. Maria would have consented to marrying Tom in the frontier custom of declaring their intent of having a religious ceremony as soon as a minister or magistrate could be found.

But as it happened, Maria was far too sick to become a bride. She was convulsed by frequent coughs, her body wracked with the ravages of consumption. Tuberculosis was often treated with isolation, and Maria's father made homespun medicine for his sick daughter, using the snake root that grew in one particular area in the Gap. But Maria's father, too, as in ill health and he begged Tom to look after his daughter. Tom pledged that he would and Maria's father soon passed away.

Tom took Maria into his care. One day, as he was out hunting for food, Maria was hoeing in a remote area by herself, searching for the root that served as her medicine. As it happened, Tom came along to where she hoed as he hunted. Animals were becoming scarce in this area, and Tom became excited, seeing the movement in the obscuring thicket. He fired without fully seeing his intended target, the bullet hitting its target with deadly accuracy, striking his sweetheart through the breast. He knelt before her as she bled out into the ground. Tom, distraught to the point of suicidal at his impetuous shot, put the barrel of the gun in his mouth with the intention of ending his life, so overcome with grief was this man. Maria, however, stopped his hand and pleaded with her dying breath that Tom that he should not put an end to his life. It was the belief that suicides could not enter Heaven, and Maria assured Tom that she would wait for him in Heaven. But Tom was so overcome with this sin that he continues to wander the area, even after death, as penance for this terrible deed.

According to Eleanor Thomas, who related this tale in her work, Community Express, "it is well attested that Tom Skelton never left the Packsaddle Gap [he] wandered the slopes of Chestnut Ridge…a wild thing who shunned the face of mankind." Eyewitnesses at the time of the canal told of mules leaping off the towpaths and shuddering in the bushes when they saw the ghostly Skelton staring from the trees. In the year 1881, it was reported that on three different occasions a conductor of a train believed they hit a man walking along the tracks. Upon searching for evidence of the impact, no body was discovered. No blood. No clothing. Nothing. It was as if the train had struck…a ghost!

Present day Packsaddle Gap.

Even today, those who manage to find their way into the area of the Packsaddle Gap to hike its hills or hunt its slopes have reported the ghostly apparition of none other than Tom Skelton, still wandering in endless self-punishment for the sin he believes he committed against the only love that had ever entered his life.

MRS. SOFFEL

This next story concerns a ghost so despised in life that a Hollywood movie was made of her. The motion picture was entitled Mrs. Soffel, which starred Diane Keaton as the titular character. Her legend begins in Allegheny County, and she was embroiled in a scandal at the start of the 20th century.

On April 12, 1901, a cold-blooded murder was committed during the commission of a robbery by the Biddle Boys and their cohorts, the Chloroform Gang, in the city of Pittsburgh. This unfortunate killing landed brothers Ed and Jack Biddle on death row in the Allegheny County jail. This was to be the end of the story of these boys, but as history will show, this was just the beginning.

Two years prior to this murder, a house was constructed in Laughlintown, a regal stone home with a servant's quarters, fish pond, and even an in-ground pool—an extravagant luxury at this fashionable time. This house was built by Pete and Kate Soffel as a place to take their children to escape the pollution that spewed forth from the steel mills, choking Victorian Pittsburgh. Also, Laughlintown was a splendid respite from the stress of Pete Soffel's job-- he was the warden of the Alleghany County jail.

Kate was interested in rehabilitating these men who were waiting for their date with the hangman, and it wasn't long before Kate was making Ed treats and bringing him reading material, including the Bible. Soon his considerable charms won her over. He was, after all, portrayed by a young Mel Gibson in the movie.

Kate soon discovered she was in love and with a doomed man. Ed gave her all the attention and affection a young wife needed and didn't get from a husband riddled with the demands of running such a facility. Ed made her feel alive. It must be remembered that Kate and her husband actually lived in the jail itself. So, in many ways, Kate was as much a captive as Ed. It was easy to sympathize with his plight. By November in 1901, escape plans began.

Kate smuggled saw blades to Ed between the pages of the Bible. She brought him black wax and chewing gum, used to reaffix the bars after they'd been cut in preparation for the time of escape. On the morning of the escape, Thursday, January 30, 1902, Kate took a page out her lover's modus operandi and lightly chloroformed her husband Pete so he could not answer the alarms. After fighting off the guards, the Biddles and Kate made their escape.

Eventually the posse caught up to the fugitives and shot Ed twice and Jack fifteen times. The Biddle Boys and Kate tried to fulfill a suicide pact before they were caught, but the attempt was unsuccessful. Jack shot himself twice in the mouth, Ed shot himself in the chest, and it's unclear whether Ed shot Kate, or she shot herself. The brothers are buried in a single grave in a Pittsburgh cemetery. But that is another story.

Kate eventually recovered from her gunshot wound, pled guilty to aiding and abetting the escape of the Biddles, and was sentenced to two years in Western Penitentiary in Pittsburgh. After she was released early for good behavior, she tried to capitalize on her infamous name by recreating her story in a play called They Died for Liberty. Later, she tried to hide from her rather unsavory notoriety by using her maiden name. Alone and humiliated, her children gone, she supported herself as a seamstress.

Kate's tale does not end there, however. She can be seen as a misty human figure that whirls and spins about, as if aimlessly searching for something that was lost and can never be found. Is her spirit's return to the vicinity of the Washington Furnace Inn an attempt to remember the happiness of the times before she met the Biddle gang?

The Ghosts of Higher Education

E ducation came first to Westmoreland County as a religious edifice to establish and promote the faith in an area that was once the frontier of civilization. The Catholic Church laid the foundation for instruction in religion as well as provided the system to train its clerics. Before long, however, the desire and need for higher education was evidenced within the general community as well.

As society became increasingly industrialized, the need for education became much more necessary than in a more agrarian culture. Westmoreland County was now on the world stage in terms of mining and steel production, and the need more a myriad of skills was increasing. Also, disposable income was now a reality, and the nouveau riches families wanted more for their children, hoping that they escape the working class culture from which they came. In this milieu, institutions of higher learning were founded throughout the region. But it seems the requisite ghosts are also included in the syllabus of a few of these schools.

St. Vincent

O nce a seminary, Saint Vincent in Latrobe is now a respected liberal arts college. The Benedictines saw education as a gift, and they wished to share this gift with the community. Now this world-class university is organized into four prestigious schools-- the Alex G. McKenna School of Business, Economics, and Government, the School of Social Sciences, Communication, and Education, the School of Humanities and Fine Arts, and the Herbert W. Boyer School of Natural Science, Mathematics, and Computing. Within this cloistered setting, however, it seems quite a few ghosts have matriculated from the afterlife.

St. Vincent College & Basilica: 2015.

The student dorms have reports of various ghostly activities, from poltergeist knocking books from shelves to the cold spots and disembodied footsteps that walk the floors of Gerard Hall. In Aurelia Hall, a poltergeist seems to have taken up residence as well. Strange noises have been reported coming from the 7th floor for decades, as well as items coming up missing and pictures being flung from the walls. One evening, several female students using a Ouija board contacted this spirit, who they claimed was named Henry. The young ladies asked him to give them a sign that he was real. It took him a while to respond, but when the girls went to bed later that night, their floor length mirror flew off the door and shattered to pieces against the opposite wall. They apologized to the poltergeist, hoping to appease the unruly spirit. To play it safe, however, they vacated their room. To this day stories persist that Henry still shows up, transitioning from a merely kinetic spirit to a full-bodied apparition with a glowing red face.

Over at St. Benedict Hall, the building is reportedly haunted by a small girl, nicknamed Jenny, who has appeared in various rooms and likes to play games and tricks on the residents, hiding their belongings and running through rooms and down halls in the middle of the night. There are also the unexplained handprints of a child on the outside of windows.

Moving out into the campus, we come to the interesting structure known as Sauerkraut Tower. This bizarrely named landmark was built in 1893, designed by Brother Wolfgang Traxler to move 80,000 gallons of water daily through the campus as a gravity-powered water tower. Not one to waste space, chief cook Brother Innocent stored barrels of pickled cabbage among its pipes in the early 20th century, earning the 90' tall building its unusual nickname. In this building, a nameless brother is said to have taken up residence. As the tale goes, this monk accidently got his clothing caught up in the windmill arms that once spun from atop the tower and was hanged. It is rumored that to this day you can still hear the monk walking the steps to the roof of the tower. And he must be afraid of the dark. Security has to frequently shut off the lights of the empty building, and some people have claimed to see his face looking out of the top window.

SETON HILL

This picturesque university sits on over 200 wooded acres, perched atop a hill with a commanding view of the city of Greensburg. It is quiet and peaceful, a haven from the bustle of the secular world that toils far below. The Sisters of Charity founded the school in 1885 as a facility for women. It was named for Elizabeth Ann Seton (1774–1821), who founded the Sisters of Charity and who, after her death, was canonized as the United States' first native-born saint. In the summer of 1882, Mother Aloysia Lowe, Mother Superior of the Pennsylvania Sisters of Charity, purchased the land in Greensburg, Pa. where Seton Hill University's main hilltop campus now stands.

The education at this school included the Seton Hill Conservatory of Music and Seton Hill Conservatory of Art, both established in 1885. In 1914, the Sisters opened the doors to Seton Hill Junior College. Four years later, in 1918, the Commonwealth of Pennsylvania approved Seton Hill's charter for a four-year institution of higher learning and Seton Hill College was born. Eventually men were allowed to attend the university when it was integrated as a coed place of learning. However, the ghosts seem to have been attending ever since the school opened its doors.

One of the most haunted locals on campus is the Administration Building. It has been said that in the early 1900s, an elderly sister fell asleep in the basement of the Motherhouse, now used as the administration building. A custodian saw her laying there and assumed she was dead. The sister was promptly given a Christian burial. However, as the legend goes, this poor old sister was not quite dead! When she woke up in a pine box, she beat on the lid of the casket until she finally passed away for real. It's said that you can hear the spirit of the nun pounding away in the Administration building late at night, trying to escape her coffin.

This main administration building is also said to be haunted by a poltergeist who has been known to open filing cabinets and scatter papers throughout a particular office. Lights have been known to go off and on, chairs have been seen rolling across the floor, and footsteps heard walking calmly across the floors. So too are disembodied voices heard calling out names of those who work in this university office building.

Seton Hill Main Entrance.

Not only does the staff have to endure hauntings, so too do the students. Brownlee Residence Hall students have reported that a mysterious purple light is seen to emanate out of nowhere, appearing in the corner of a dorm room on the first floor. Also, it's been reported that the shadow of girl who had allegedly hanged herself many years ago in her room can be seen on the wall across from the room that it supposedly happened.

The sleeping arrangements at Maura Hall seem to be just as haunted. This residence building dates back to 1908, and within its walls, the spirits of the old teaching nuns have been reported roaming its corridors, seen as ghostly apparitions wearing their full habit.

Even the main parking lot at Seton Hill is said to be haunted. There have been reports that the ephemeral ghost of a priest has been seen crossing the main lot during the evening hours.

UNIVERSITY OF PITTSBURGH AT GREENSBURG

This branch from the main campus of the University of Pittsburgh was founded in 1963 when area school superintendents requested a branch for area students to avoid relocation out of Westmoreland County and into the city of Pittsburgh. The university's first building, Vogel Hall, welcomed the initial class into its halls. Although it is not one of the older colleges, it still has its history of hauntings.

Lynch Hall at University of Pitt-Greensburg: Michael G. White, 2008.

The Lynch Hall building was originally built in 1922 as a private residence. Acquired by the university in 1964, it now houses administrative offices. Security guards have claimed to have spotted a ghost in the building, with one guard claiming that it is the spirit of the homes first occupant, Commander Lynch. Not only does Lynch act as a poltergeist pulling pranks, but he's decidedly unhappy about confinement within his former home. Two students at the university mustered a group of ghost hunting students into the Lynch basement and had a little chat with Commander Lynch via a Ouija board. He confirmed he was the spirit haunting the house and went on to communicate that he was stuck in his old residence, because of, as he put it, "Death." Then Lynch unceremoniously told the students to "Get Out!"

Rossetti Hall also has its resident ghost. This haunting is another legacy of the Lynch family, for Rossetti Hall was the home of the Commander's daughter, Mary Quinn. Rossetti Hall is now the admissions office. Strange noises and events have occurred there, allegedly committed by the ghost of Mary Quinn. Research teams have photographed orbs, and the full-bodied apparition of a young lady in an elegant gown has been seen within Rossetti Hall.

Hauntings of the Holy

C hurches are supposedly the sanctuary from all things haunting, are they not? They are the conclaves against supernatural forces, right? In Westmoreland County, this assumption is not always accurate. While most churches are peaceful places of prayer and contemplation, a few are harbingers of things not so holy.

St. Joseph's Chapel at Seton Hill

T he college is reportedly haunted, so why not the accompanying chapel? Built in 1896 as part of the original Motherhouse, St. Joseph's Chapel is located on the third floor of the Administration building.

Seton Hill St. Joseph's Chapel Interior: Kayla Sawyer, 2009.

This small church appears to be the residence of the transparent apparition of a nun who haunts in the room next to the organ. The organ door, it has be said, will open and close on its own, and a chorus of ghostly voices singing and phantom music coming from the otherwise empty chapel can be heard from time to time.

To further compile this haunting, there's the legend of a student who became so depressed that she went to the bell tower, which is entered through the chapel, and threw herself off into the courtyard below, committing suicide. Her ghost is said to be seen around campus. Sometimes her ghost is seen reliving the tragic event, a shimmering figure appears at the window then steps out only to disappear on impact with the concrete below. Maybe the chapel is a place of perpetual penance for the girl who was so depressed she took her own life.

ST. VINCENT'S CHURCH

An interesting intelligent haunting in a college in Westmoreland County involves a ghostly monk at St. Vincent. Saint Vincent Parish was founded in 1790. It was the first Catholic parish in Pennsylvania west of the Allegheny Mountains. All that history has apparently stored some fascinating hauntings within its sacred stone walls.

In the early fall of 1859, the ghost of a Benedictine began haunting the church that stood on the grounds. For over a month the ghost appeared to a novice in the novice's bedroom. More spectacularly, this same ghost manifested during Mass and preached that the teachings on Purgatory were false. It should be pointed out that the Vatican did indeed eventually change its position on the validity of Purgatory. The last reported sighting of this ghostly monk was in 1936, when it appeared to two men on a road winding through the abbey grounds.

Soon the need for a larger church was necessary, and the cornerstone of the basilica was laid in 1892. But it seems this magnificent structure also has its hauntings as well. Certain people say they can feel the presence of others within its walls, even when the basilica is completely empty. It may be the spirits of a few deceased monks, whose apparitions have been seen from time to time, their ghosts kneeling in prayer. Yearly, security guards at the University have reported hearing unusual noises echoing from within the basilica after midnight Mass on Christmas Eve. They have reported hearing the sound of kneelers going down, the sweet smell of incense, and the angelic sounds of music and singing.

The famous founder of St. Vincent is even seen on occasion, apparently making a visit from his respite in the afterlife. Abbot Boniface, the founder of the college, rises on the anniversary of his December 8th death and goes to the basilica to say mass for the souls of the departed. He passes through every red door in the crypt area where he's buried beneath the church to check on everyone and to find out how the school has progressed over the years. He's the most famous spirit at St. Vincent, and his sighting is jokingly referred to as "freshman orientation" on campus.

ST. JOSEPH'S ROMAN CATHOLIC CHURCH

St. Joseph's Roman Catholic Church is a utilitarian built in 1959. A Catholic school was built above the sanctuary because at this time a Catholic education was considered paramount in promoting the faith. The church was the middle floor of the building, a religious space capable of holding 300 parishioners. Below, in the basement, was the school's cafeteria and lunchroom that served additionally as a social hall, a gym for the students, and a bingo parlor one day a week. This very unassuming church seems too insignificant to be the epicenter of anything traumatic. However, this church and its grounds was the site of an event that shocked this little town.

St. Joseph's Roman Catholic Church, Derry, PA: 2015.

It has been said that the town of Derry collectively has post-traumatic stress syndrome from one event that occurred on Labor Day, September 5th, 1978. A church bazaar had a helicopter fly over as a young girl dropped ping-pong balls out of the door. People gathered under the helicopter in the hopes of grabbing a lucky numbered ball. Then the unthinkable happened—the helicopter stalled and fell into the crowd. One witness described the hellish scene as "running with rivers of blood." Six persons were killed instantly when the helicopter slammed into a concession stand at St. Joseph's Catholic Church. A seventh died soon after. Around 800 people, over half the current population of Derry, were present in the confined space of the 10,000 square foot parking lot. The basement of the church, then used as the cafeteria for the school attached to the church, was used as a makeshift morgue.

Indiana Gazette Headline of Derry Copter Crash: Indiana Gazette, 1978.

Sadly, not even a plaque of memorial marks the site, even though this tragic event single-handedly changed the aviation rules regarding the use of helicopters. But the weeping specters seen in the parking lot of the church, figures as dark as the night, hunched over in what has been described as "profound sadness," convey the terror, horror, and exasperating loss in such a way that they may be the only memorial needed for this unspeakable event.

St. Martin's Roman Catholic Church

The last haunted church to be investigated is actually the mother church to St. Joseph's. On the grounds of this church, those who perished in the various train accidents that plagued this railroad town are interred, as well as those who succumbed to the vicious terrorism of the Black Hand. It holds within its consecrated and hallowed grounds miners and quarry men, immigrants and quarryman. Buried in its cemetery are also the victims of the helicopter that accidentally crashed into the bazaar of its sister church, St. Joseph's. St. Martin's has been the unfortunate repository of all things tragic that has occurred in the town of Derry through the years.

St. Martin's Church in Derry: 2015.

St. Martin's was built in New Derry in the year 1856, constructed by the Irish and German immigrants to this area, built with bricks made from the land itself. It was raised to replace Mt. Carmel, a church about five miles from the town of New Derry. This old Mt. Carmel church has burned numerous times, caused by careless splashing of the kerosene used to illuminate the interior of the wooden structure. St. Martin's was built strong, with the deliberate intention that this new church would withstand the years. It still has the original tin roof and the sanctuary is painted an odd red, the color called Pompey Red. This hue is a unique color, first unearthed during the excavation of the ancient Roman city of Pompey preserved under the ash from Mt. Vesuvius. The 1850s and 60s was indeed a time of war and instability, but it was also the time of rediscovery and exploration, and this little church is a testament to that, using Pompey Red to decorate its most sacred area. Even after a sanctuary fire in 1963, this little country church still stands like a preserved time capsule, serving the faithful of this Westmoreland County community.

A ghostly figure has indeed been seen at St Martin's. This church has witnessed sightings of a lady dressed in all black with long, pure white hair. The curious feature --or lack thereof-- is this apparition appears to lack eyes! This wrinkle-faced ghost has been spotted hovering around Saint Martin's Church, a site not far from Barr Fort and the mining towns of Pandora and Atlantic where hot smoke once spewed into the air. Is she a demon, tormented by the religious edifice so close to the bloody battle-ground of Barr Fort? Is she the spectral personification of the evil of the Black Hand? Or is this ghost, in such despair of witnessing so many violent deaths and horrific accidents, no longer wanting eyes to see any more of the terrible events of this world?

One local witness described this ghost in this way: "I remember when I was little girl around the age of 7 or 8 and I lived on a farm that sits right off Route 982 in New Derry and I looked out my first floor bedroom window and saw this same white haired old lady wearing all black and carrying a cane. I didn't know until I was older that there was a cemetery near there and that someone else encountered the same thing." This ghost seems to be closely associated with death, giving off the vibe that it is inextricably tied with the loss of life.

Interestingly enough, the road that fronts St. Martin's—Route 982— was the way formerly known as "the Hollow," where so many murdered victims were unceremoniously dumped by the Black Hand. While some see this manifestation as a demon, many more feel as if this phantom is a creation manifested from the turmoil of this area. To some researchers, it seems this ghost not so much torments this area but mourns its history.

THE WITCH'S CURSE:
THE GHOST TOWN OF LIVERMORE

Ever since William Penn presided over the state's only official witch trial in 1684, witchcraft and folk magic have been a part of the history of the Keystone State. Besides the ghost of the witch reported to be the denizen of the Witch's Tunnel, Westmoreland County also boasts another interesting place called Livermore.

Livermore Station, 1908.

It seems that there was a certain woman who lived near this small village along the Conemaugh River in the late 1700s. She was accused of consorting with the Devil himself and sentenced to death. According to the legend, she was burned at the stake for her crimes against God. But as the flames lapped at her skin, she cursed the town, assuring them that one hundred years after her death—to the day—flood waters would consume the area in the same way fire consumed her mortal body. A century after her death, a flood did indeed inundate the land. We call this deluge the Johnstown Flood!

Livermore was once a prosperous town built around the railroad and mining industry. It had a busy train station and a hotel in its heyday. For those who resided in Livermore, the town had a school, baseball team, church, and residential homes. That is until it first flooded in 1889. It was such a ferocious inundation that a legend says that a witch had inhabited this town over a century ago. The residents, fearing her magic and communication with the devil, took it into their own hands to rid themselves of her. It was said they burned the witch at the stake, sending her and her influence to Hell. But as she succumbed to the flames, it was said she cursed the town. She stated that these flames would be quenched by a flood on the anniversary of her death. On May 31st 1889, her prophecy came true. The same flood that destroyed Johnstown also washed away Livermore. The destruction was so terrible that the only logical conclusion was a witch's curse must be behind such hellish force of nature.

JOHNSTOWN FLOOD, MAY 31st, 1889.

LOSS FROM 10,000 TO 12,000 LIVES.

Johnstown Flood Damage: Histed, 1889: Library of Congress.

VERITABLE VALLEY OF DEATH

Latest Particulars of the Johnstown Disaster Confirm the Worst Previous Reports.

THE DEAD WILL NUMBER AT LEAST 8,000,

And $11,000,000 Will Hardly Begin to Replace the Property Swept Away by the Awful Deluge.

FIRE ADDS ITS TERRORS TO THE SCENE,

Burning to Death Seven Hundred People, Who Had Sought Refuge on Drift Heaps or Wrecked Houses.

THE RIVER BANKS LINED WITH CORPSES,

While Hundreds More Float With the Current in a Never-Ending Procession of Death.

PASSENGER TRAINS ARE ANNIHILATED

And Their Hundreds of Occupants Hurled Into Eternity Without a Moment's Warning,

THE CARRION CROWS BEGIN TO COME,

Plucking at the Bodies as They Are Whirled Along on the Bosom of the Foaming Torrent.

VULTURES IN HUMAN FORM COME ALSO·

They Steal the Valuables of the Dead, and Even Strip the Bodies of Their Clothing.

NO. 153.

VOL. XI.

Daily Globe.

ST. PAUL

SUNDAY ISSUE.

SAINT PAUL, MINN., SUNDAY MORNING, JUNE 2, 1889.—SIXTEEN PAGES.

Headline from Minneapolis Daily Globe, Johnstown Flood: 1889. Library of Congress.

But the flood of 1889 was no less devastating without the involvement of a witch. The deluge rendered the Juniata Branch of the Pennsylvania Canal useless, stranding the Western Division from commerce in the east; canal towns, such as Livermore, began a steady decline. Livermore especially, isolated by its location, was cut off from the rest of the area. But the Conemaugh River on which the town was situated created more havoc to the already faltering town.

Between March 16 and 21, 1936, the tributaries of the Allegheny and Monongahela Rivers including the Conemaugh flooded because of heavy rainfall and melting snow and ice. The area had been experiencing extremely cold temperatures, and in many places, the ground was frozen solid to a depth of four feet, preventing water from soaking into the ground. Residents of Livermore and the other low-lying towns of Westmoreland County such as Cokeville and Bairdstown were evacuated by rowboats in the evening of March 17, many gathering at higher ground. "The Great St. Patrick's Day Flood" submerged Livermore under 18 feet of water, sweeping away the bridge spanning the Conemaugh and fourteen buildings, while others were ruined or severely damaged. Floodwaters destroyed eight homes, four properties, three barns, two garages, and the stocks of both general stores. The flood caused one fatality in Livermore. As a whole, the flood claimed about 80 lives and caused the region over $500 million in damages. No wonder people thought this place was cursed.

In 1952, the town was forever buried under water as a precaution that such an event would never happen again. But the memory of the imagined curse lingers. To this day, Livermore is sometimes called Satan's Seat, as if a tangible evil resides here. And maybe it does. Paranormal investigators have reported a slew of activity, and psychics have witnessed many ghosts throughout the site of the former town.

A demonic entity is said to haunt the fringes of the former railroad tracks, now converted into walking path in a section of the West Penn Trail. It has been seen as a slumped over shadowy figure, more animal than man. It walks with its knuckles to the ground, its eyes burning red like the flames that allegedly consumed the witch. On several occasions, it has been reported stalking those who trespass into its domain at night, lurking in the darkness, following closely behind. It has even been heard snarling a vicious bestial warning to those brave enough to leave the parking lot and venture into the depths of Livermore at night.

As if a guardian of the land, a Native American has been seen in the same area as the phantom beast. By all accounts, this ghost is a protective spirit, centuries older than the first white settlement. One psychic researcher referred to him as "Monogehelian." This is the original culture that occupied this area but mysteriously vanished before the presence of the first white man into the area that came to be known as Westmoreland County. This ghost is described as visually quite handsome, with long black hair and a chiseled face with strong features. He is dressed in buckskin and wears a shell necklace around his neck. He has been seen wandering through the desolate regions of this place, perhaps endlessly stalking the demon that is said to reside here.

But these are not the only ghosts along this trail. Indeed, ghost trains are seen on numerous occasions. One often scares walkers off the trail, its light piercing the night as it races silently toward them, only to vanish before reaching them. Another ghost train, this one much more ominous, has been witnessed racing along the tracks that are still in use. This train glows an eerie green as is rushes along in a swirling fog, blocking the only egress from Livermore. Witnesses have been stricken with terror as the ghost train, filled with ghoulish passengers whose faces are no more than rotting corpses, block their only exit.

A house, possibly the former residence of the supposed witch, has also been seen at Livermore, but never appearing in the same area. When approached, the house simply disappears.

HAUNTED THEATRES

As the small towns of Westmoreland County prospered through the business of coal, coke, and the railroad, they eventually grew into urban centers. To flaunt their new wealth, many of these towns built theatres as cultural centers to show the world that they were not working class communities but urbane, enlightened cultural centers.

Scottdale, PA: 1910. Courtesy Brown Street Clock Registry.

This Westmoreland County borough was named Scottdale in honor of Col. Thomas A. Scott, who was assistant secretary of war during the Civil War and later president of the Pennsylvania Railroad when it opened its Scottdale branch in the spring of 1873. The town was incorporated on February 5, 1874. The railroad along with the coal and coke industry played a prominent role in the prosperity and development of this community. The Pennsylvania Railroad and Baltimore and Ohio Railroad each built branch lines through the community in the early 1870s. With the coming of the railroads, the community's economy shifted from agriculture to manufacturing and mining. By the early 1900s, there were 30,000 coke ovens in this area, and Scottdale was centrally located with hundreds of mining companies surrounding it. The railroad was used to transport coal and coke to the various industrial markets throughout the country. This situation brought in a staggering amount of revenue into this town. Amazingly, at the dawn of the 20th century, there were more millionaires per capita in Scottdale than in any other city in the United States!

This period of wealth and affluence left an indelible mark on the town that is evidenced by the grandeur of the historic homes and buildings located in and around the town. The present day town of Scottdale is home to unique boutiques and cozy restaurants, a mere shadow of its former prosperity. But there are reminders of the civic opulence of the town, most notably in the guise of their historic opera house that offers live theatrical productions.

THE GEYER PERFORMING ARTS CENTER

The Geyer Performing Arts Center is now a community theater located in Scottdale. Build in 1900, during the heyday of the town, the theatre fell into disuse as the economy evolved out of its railroad and coal reliance, and Scottdale fell out of favor. However, the Geyer Theater was reopened in 1988, and from the ghosts seen in this grand hall, apparently to an appreciative audience—both dead and alive. These full-bodied apparitions have been seen quite frequently in this majestic venue, sometimes during one of the various performances, other times when the house is dark. But this haunting is always reported in the same way—an elderly couple, presumably husband and wife, are seated toward the rear of the hall, their gaze cast forward, toward the stage. These two spirits may have been long-time theatre goers, simply returning out of habit to the Geyer, a place they were fond of in life. Even in death, these two ghosts still have the occasional date night.

The most prominent spook is that of John Bixler, one of the early owners of the Theater, who's been spotted in a smart white suit on the balcony, watching the stage (and probably counting the house).

Geyer Performing Arts Center, Scottdale: 2012.

Another spirit has been dubbed Mary, a young girl that likes to create a bit of havoc with the lighting. Other workers have heard voices calling their names in an otherwise empty building. According to a psychic, this young girl was playing aimlessly back stage and climbed the ladder to the catwalk. Unable to keep her balance, she slipped and fell to her death on the stage far below. She seems to have been here ever since.

APPLE HILL PLAYHOUSE

The Apple Hill Playhouse, however, has a ghost who is not keen on seeing the show; indeed, this spirit seems to indicate that it misses the limelight! The Apple Hill Playhouse is located in the busy highway town of Delmont. Delmont was initially known as Salem Crossroads. Several areas in and around the borough still carry the Salem reference. Major navigational roads were built through the area in the late 1700s, and what is now local Route 66 was built in 1800. The Northern Turnpike was completed in 1818, which formed the "crossroads". Delmont was a busy stagecoach stop until trains replaced stagecoaches in the 1850s. Aside from the historical genesis of the town as a toll intersection and stagecoach stop, one of Delmont's notable characteristics is that it is the meeting point of two major highways, U.S. Route 22 and State Route 66.

This place was initially known as New Salem, named in 1785 when 300 acres of land were sold to William Wilson. Major navigational roads were built through this area in the late 18th century, and what is now local Route 66 was built in 1800. Soon the East-West Northern Turnpike was completed in 1819 linking Philadelphia to Pittsburgh. Because of these road construction projects, Delmont was a busy stagecoach stop boasting at one time five stage coach lines through the village. Travelers would be brought here tired and hungry and they would indulge in the services of the several inns and taverns in this town. Coach travel would not last long, however. In 1853, the Pennsylvania Railroad was complete through Westmoreland County to Pittsburgh. This was a far faster and more economical way to travel, not to mention much safer for those making the journey. In 1855, the last stagecoach passed through Delmont ending the stagecoach era for this crossroads town. But the highways continued to funnel revenue into this area; and unlike other towns that relied so heavily on the rails, Delmont was able to survive.

The Apple Hill Playhouse, Delmont, PA: Apple Hill Playhouse, 2016.

And so too has this town's playhouse. Since 1962, Apple Hill Playhouse in has continued to provide professional productions and top-notch dinner theatre. "It all began more than half a century ago," explained Pat Beyer, the Executive Producer and owner of Apple Hill Playhouse. "The renovated barn which comprises the main theatre building was part of a local farm and has a pre-civil war history. It even housed mules used to work the local mines, but in 1952, with the last of the mule leavings scrubbed away, an aspiring country theatre was born. For ten years it was the William Penn Playhouse, becoming Apple Hill after a change in ownership in 1962."

Each season, nearly 100 actors ply their craft on the stage of the Apple Hill Playhouse. This is a venue where imagination takes flight. Audiences get lost in the world of the stage, a welcomed two-hour break from life. It has been said, live theatre has no substitute. Apparently, the dead think so as well.

Various performers from different shows throughout the years have told tales of a disruptive ghost who haunts the dressing rooms of this playhouse. Not only are props and scripts thrown and scattered, but reflections of a shadow are frequently witnessed passing by in the mirrors. There is an icy feeling when this entity enters the backstage area, giving actors and directors the feeling that an unhappy reviewer is throwing their weight around. It seems even ghosts can be critics.

CASINO THEATRE

This area at the edge of Westmoreland County was the site of labor unrest early in its history. In the 1890s, the Apollo Iron and Steel Company ended a bitterly contested workers' dispute by hiring replacements from the surrounding countryside. To avoid future unrest, however, the company sought to gain tighter control over its workers not only at the factory but also in their homes. Drawing upon a philosophy of reform movements in Europe and the United States, the firm decided that providing workers with good housing and a good urban environment would make them more loyal and productive. In 1895, Apollo Iron and Steel built a new, integrated, non-unionized steelworks and hired the nation's preeminent landscape architectural firm, Olmsted, Olmsted and Eliot, to design the model industrial town that came to be known as Vandergrift. Part of this urban vision was to provide entertainment for the masses. This led to the construction of the Casino Theatre.

Municipal Building, Vandergrift, Pa.

Postcard featuring the Casino Theater, Vandergrift, PA: photographer unknown.

The Casino Theatre was built in 1900 and named after the second Broadway theatre in New York City. The Casino came to be the town's showpiece. The Casino was fashioned in the opulently ornate Greek Revival Style. The theatre's most distinctive and historic feature is its temple front with four Greek Ionic columns. The Casino theatre had an orchestra pit and a well-appointed balcony. From its inception up until 1927, this theatre hosted live entertainment and was a popular stop along the Vaudeville Circuit. Among its historic visitors during the past century were President William H. Taft, world boxing champion Bob Fitsimmons, composer Hoagy Carmichael, the Lone Ranger, Tex Ritter and the Three Stooges. But change was in the air. Touring entertainment gave way to the motion picture. This theatre adapted with the times. In 1927, the Casino was remodeled as Westmoreland County's largest movie theater. The first show was "The Robe", a Biblical spectacular. In the 1950s, the theater was converted to show wide-screen movies to compete with the new sensation—television. The Casino Theatre showed its last movie in 1981 and remained dark for more ten years after. The theater reopened in 1996. The League of Historic American theatre's lists the Casino Theatre as the fourth oldest operating theatre in Pennsylvania.

Whether the entity lingers in anticipation of the next Hollywood movie projection or a performance from Vaudevillians like the Three Stooges is uncertain; but the ghost of the Casino Theatre waits in the balcony, dressed in Victorian splendor complete with a fashionably wide brimmed hat, enduring the dark silence, serene in her seat in this grand hall. She has been seen by many who have visited this theatre, and she has become a fixture in this grand building.

PALACE THEATRE

After the end of the Revolutionary War, an inn was built along a wagon trail that stretched from Philadelphia west over the Appalachian Mountains to Fort Pitt, now the city of Pittsburgh. Eventually a tiny settlement known as Newtown grew around this inn, which would have been located today at the very center the modern business district. Newtown eventually was renamed Greensburg after Nathanael Greene, a major general of the Continental Army in the American Revolutionary War.

Palace Theatre, Greensburg, PA.

The Palace Theatre has been a major force in Westmoreland County's cultural scene for generations. Opened September 2, 1926, as the Manos Theatre, The Palace Theatre today hosts the widest variety of live entertainment in the area in a beautifully renovated 1369-seat facility, located across from the reportedly haunted county courthouse at 21 West Otterman Street in downtown Greensburg. And this theatre seems to have a protective spirit still haunting the auditorium.

Jess McGovern was a 14-year employee of the Palace Theatre, one of a dedicated, yet small, staff that worked varied hours and performed any and all tasks required to keep a theatre operational. This included the tech work. She and the staff had often felt as if they were not alone in this theatre, and from time to time would hear the sounds of footsteps in empty halls and on the darkened stage. Ms. McGovern had a mantra, "We know you are here and you know we are here so let's get along." Even though lights would turn off and on by themselves and papers would be moved from desks and stacked in other places, the relationship between the living and the dead was not confrontational.

One particular evening, Ms. McGovern was asked to do some repair work on a lighting rig. The rig was held by airline cables 60 feet in the air over the stage. McGovern dutifully began climbing the ladder that ascended to the catwalk when she heard movement above her. Off to the side, she saw a figure. Assuming it was another worker, McGovern hollered out a "hello," which was met with no response. But the shadow figure was still there, and it made its way out onto the catwalk. Looking up at the figure, McGovern saw that it was a black figure with no face. The entity then proceeded to unknot the tangle in the wires of the lighting. McGovern, still watching in amazement from the ladder, offered an astonished "thank you." The dark figure nodded and dropped back, becoming one with the surrounding darkness.

Returning to the office, McGovern's boss said, "It looks like you saw a ghost" by the drawn expression on her employee's face. McGovern told her boss of her encounter, and suspecting a prank, followed McGovern to the stage. There they discovered the lighting rig untangled, thanks to the "caretaker of the Palace."

GEM THEATRE

Gem Theater, a grand movie house opened in 1916. After the business of operatic movie-going went out of vogue and the building began to crumble in disrepair, area teens would break in through the back and conduct ritual séances, attempting to summon "the other side." The place was old, abandoned, and not without terminal creepiness. This was an ideal spot for unwitting teens to perform misguided rituals, attempting to contact the other side. In one particular case that occurred in 1999, the respondent may have been from Hell!

Historic Gem Theatre Facade, Derry, PA: Courtesy Derry Area Historical Society.

The small group of teens gathered in the cavernous darkness of the Gem Theater, lit a single black candle (they did this because a book they had purchased suggested it would draw spirits, like a moth to the flame), and, using a Ouija board, attempted to conjure the spirit world. This time it seems as if a portal was opened and a "red glowing demon" sprang from the Ouija board, flew through the air, circled the room, and disappeared. The teens (now all adults, a couple even respected members of the community) ran from the place, leaving their spirit board behind, their black candle extinguished by the whoosh of the demon as it flew about the room. They reported this entity as a "demon" because that was "the vibe" they got. It was as if their minds were informed by the nature of this spirit. One witness said they were on their knees in church the very next Sunday. Another witness, who is now a young woman and seemingly struggling emotionally, said that her impression was that the demon wasn't necessarily summoned by the ritual, but already resided in the building. She felt as if the group provided the energy it needed to materialize, and it simply drew from that energy to manifest. "And then it was gone," she said. One must wonder, where did this demon go?

Gem Theatre Ticket, Derry, PA: Courtesy Derry Area Historical Society.

GREENSBURG COURTHOUSE

T he Westmoreland County Courthouse is one of the tallest structures in Greensburg, standing a commanding 175 feet above street level and designed by William Kauffman in a Beaux Arts style. The current building is the county's fourth courthouse and was constructed in 1906. The first courthouse was used from 1787 to 1801. The second courthouse was demolished in 1854 and the third demolished in 1901.

The current courthouse is built on the site of the old county jail, which was in use from the early 1900s to the 1960s. It seems events of the past haunt this structure, an innocent ghost still reminding those working in the courthouse of the injustice from the past. Dispatchers in what was then the 911 call center have seen the translucent image of the lower part of a man hanging on a video security monitor. The camera was pointing toward the hallway in the upper parking level, leading from the magistrate's office toward the delivery garage area. When they went to the area to investigate the image on the security monitor, they saw nothing; however, they felt coldness in the area, and were seen to pass through the image on the camera as they checked the area. Could this be the spectral reminder of the hanging of Joseph Evans?

April 20, 1830 was the date of the very first and last public execution in Greensburg. Spectators came in wagons, on horseback and on foot, from all sections of the county and from all the surrounding counties. Many came of foot a distance of thirty miles to witness the execution. The country people seemed to abandon their work at home and make long journeys in order to be present.

Greensburg, PA County Courthouse, 2015.

At the time of his execution, Evans was about twenty-two years old. In 1829, while the Pennsylvania canal was under construction, he came to our country as a day laborer, on the part of it that passed through Derry Township. One Sunday evening he had a dispute with a man about stealing a pair of shows, but they became good friends again over a pint of apple brandy. On the night before Christmas, he amused himself by whistling "Boyne Water," in the presence of three Irishmen who at once attacked him vigorously. Evans fought, defending himself and with success, but from that came his undoing. On the day before New Year, he and others were preparing for the approaching holiday by drinking whisky and playing cards. Evans was in company with Cissler and with the Irish with whom he had quarreled. A general fight soon ensued, in which Evans was almost alone, for he was unpopular and disliked by most of his associates. To defend himself he seized a shovel, and swung it back and forth before him to keep them away from him. Cissler was not in the fight against Evans at all, but interposed to stop the quarrel. Unfortunately, he came too near and received a blow in the forehead from Evans' shovel. Cissler fell heavily and struck the back of his head on an iron kettle. Whether he was killed by striking his head against the kettle or by the blow of the shovel is not known; but he breathed only a few times and died without speaking another word.

Evans was thus blamed and made a violent attempt to escape. A large crowd surrounded him and attempted to tie him, but Evans fought them off until the mob began to beat him into submission. Then he was taken to Bairdstown for a hearing before Squire Scott, upon whose commitment he was lodged in jail in Greensburg, on January 2, 1830. In the following February Evans was tried before Judge John Young, and found guilty of murder in the first degree.

On April 14, 1830, Evans made a confession, or, more properly speaking, a statement, that was published in the Westmoreland Republican, issued April 23, 1830. From this statement it is learned that he was naturally of a wild disposition, but perhaps no worse than his rowdy associates. He confessed that he had repeatedly engaged in fights, and had assisted in tarring and feathering two disreputable men, then riding them on a rail. He also shaved the mane and tail of a horse belonging to a Methodist preacher, and he says that he so "lathered" the preacher that he was laid up for two weeks. He protested very emphatically against some of the evidence, and affirmed that much of the evidence was entirely false. Sadly, Evans' statement probably contained much more truth than the testimony against him. However, he was tried in the court of public opinion and convicted of being a cold-blooded murderer. He was sentenced to death by hanging.

With his last words, Evans asserted his innocence of intending to kill any one, and, least of all, Cissler. He again stated that great injustice was done him by the witnesses against him, whom he forgave. After he was hanged, his body was interred under the gallows, but it is a local legend that his body was taken from the grave the night following.

THE
REGISTER OF PENNSYLVANIA.

DEVOTED TO THE PRESERVATION OF EVERY KIND OF USEFUL INFORMATION RESPECTING THE STATE.

EDITED BY SAMUEL HAZARD.

VOL. V.—NO. 19.   PHILADELPHIA, MAY 8, 1830.   NO. 123.

GREENSBURGH, April 28.
The Execution. On Tuesday last, about three o'clock P. M. the sentence of the law was executed on the unfortunate Joseph Evans, for the murder of John Cissler, being the first execution since the seat of justice was established in this place, upwards of 40 years.

Evans Execution, Register of Pennsylvania: Samuel Hazard, 1830.

Torrance State Hospital

orrance State hospital is situated on a parcel of land very near the site where the Wallace Fort stood. It was built upon a slight rise above the Conemaugh River that winds itself through the Packsaddle Gap. If any place were to be chosen as a building site in an area of concentrated paranormal activity, it would be the place chosen for the hospital at Torrance.

In 1917, well before the main hospital buildings were constructed, the Crabb farm had a cow barn that was used as the first building to house mental patients at this location. Treatment for mental conditions was in its infancy, and as can be imagined, treatment in a barn built to shelter livestock was less than adequate. As this was the time of the flu epidemic, many patients succumbed to the outbreak. Realizing that a better-equipped facility was needed, the construction of the main hospital campus began. 2,400 acres of land was purchased and the building of the facilities commenced. Thirty treatment and residential buildings were constructed, as well as homes for the doctors who lived on site.

Torrance State Hospital Panorama, 2015.

The mental facility opened to patients on November 25, 1919. The Western State Hospital for the Insane was the title first used for the mental facility. In 1923, the hospital became known as Torrance State Hospital. For its time, Torrance was a modern facility and practiced up to date medical methods for the treatment of mental disorders. Bear in mind, however, that the treatment of mental illness was still quite barbaric at this time and in a relative immaturity as a medical field. Lobotomies were regularly performed, rendering the patient, in many cases, vegetative. And, of course, the horrors of shock treatments undoubtedly unleashed anguished energies into this area. But the hospital was ahead of its time in that it broke from the traditional configuration of contemporary mental facilities. Most asylums were built to function as part of the confined Kirkbride system, a treatment plan where the very architecture of a hospital was believed to help the patient rehabilitate. But housing and treatment was done under one roof. Torrance, on the other hand, was built as part of the Cottage Plan. This Cottage Plan was a derivation of a Victorian convention where multiple institutional buildings with long, rambling wings formed a campus-like setting. Following this plan, Torrance also incorporated farmlands as part of the treatment of its patients. Torrance was a self-contained community, isolated from the nearest town by miles. Work was considered an essential part of therapy. The patients planted and harvested their own crops in the massive fields that encircled the hospital grounds. Animals were raised and slaughtered on site. Torrance boasted a large piggery, a cannery, and its own laundry. Horses were kept and cared for as needed transportation to pull the carts and haul the wagons. This self-sufficiency was needed--through the 1950s and '60s, the inpatient population was over 3,300!

Abandoned wing in the Cottage Plan, now overgrown.

Nature was also seen as an indispensable form of therapy. With its secluded setting and bucolic environment, this was a readily available rehabilitation. The admitted were allowed to walk the grounds, which had tree-lined lanes and wooded groves. And it seems as if this form of therapy continues even after death.

Spirits are still witnessed walking the grounds, out of either residual habit or intelligent intent. However, it is not wise to invade their space or interfere with their strolls. Cars have been known to stall when approaching an apparition, and sometimes mischievous pranks are carried out by unseen hands, such as turning windshield wipers backwards. As inviting as it may seem to join these spirits on their walk, it is better to let them go about on their own.

In the long history of the hospital, Torrance aided not only the mentally ill. During the St. Patrick's Day Flood of 1936, Torrance took in refugees from the high waters that raged through this area of Westmoreland County. With power supplies washed away, Torrance was a haven for the displaced. The nearest town, Cokeville, lost the bridge connecting it to the closest town, so the hospital was a refuge to those who watched their town swept into the river.

In 1953, tuberculosis patients began to be admitted to the Graff Building. Death was a daily occurrence during this epidemic. All the pain and agony, congealing into an energy, seems to have embedded itself into this hospital building. Maybe this is the reason that this particular site is supposedly the most haunted of all the buildings on the Torrance campus. Today this cottage decays and crumbles, its walls covered with spray-painted graffiti. No trespassing signs nailed to the trees and gates close off the only road that serves as access to the Graff Building. But ghost hunters bold enough to ignore the very real possibility of a criminal trespass charge have reported the unnerving presence of a little girl at this site. Most of the time she makes herself known only through faint laughter, but on occasion some intrepid teams have had terrifying encounters with the spirit. Sometimes she can be seen leering from the broken glass of one of the windows in the Renner building, watching as people walk down its dirt road that leads to the building. It has been reported that she will tap on windows. Once inside, the apparition has manifested to some eyewitnesses and motioned for them to follow her. She attempts to lead them into a room in which the floor has caved in. If her attempts to lure you are refused, she smiles an evil grin and disappears. Some psychics feel that she is not actually the spirit of a deceased little girl but rather a demonic entity that has taken on the form of a little girl to lure trespassers into who knows what! If ever you find yourself in an abandoned mental facility in the dead of night and a little girl in a tidy little dress materializes out of this air and asks you to follow her, it is a good bet that you should leave. Immediately!

But these are not the only places on the campus of Torrance State Hospital that has reported ghostly activity. The grand Administration Building, the scene of four decades of kinetic hospital activity, seems to have had the ability to store some of this activity within its walls. Loud noises and the incomprehensible sounds of distant conversation have been widely reported. Elevators have even been known to open at will along with doors slamming throughout the empty building. Witnesses have said it was as if you stepped into a fully operating facility, with all the buzz of activity around you. The only difference is that the building was completely empty! Orbs have been photographed in this building, a possible glimpse at the otherworldly energy that still occupies this space.

The Boiler House, with its imposing brick smoke stack, has reports of silvery shadows wisping like spectral fog moving throughout the building's bowels. The echoing sounds of men working, heavy hammers pounding on metal, and the harsh scraping of steel on cold stone was been heard on numerous occasions. It is as if all the residual energies associated with construction and maintaining of this structure continues even to this day.

Another abandoned out-building on the Torrance campus.

The Diefert Building was once the residence hall where many patients had lived through the years. Now it is abandoned. However, it seems that at least one resident still resides in her old room at the end of the hall. Even before it closed its doors, nurses reported seeing the ghost of an elderly woman who had died years earlier walking the halls of this building. There was nothing terrifying about her presence, all reports indicate, just a startling jolt of seeing a transparent woman moving past your desk at three in the morning. Sometimes the sound of her rocking chair was heard in the dead of night, coming from behind the door of a then vacant room where the woman once lived. When the noise was investigated, nothing was discovered.

The other buildings stand empty and slowly rotting, the history of this facility crumbling every day. The majority of the hospital began closing in the late 1960s, and now the campus stands testament to the medical procedures of the past. Most buildings are sealed off from any prying eyes brave enough to trespass into the hospital's grounds. It seems as if Torrance has any more secrets or ghosts, they are kept well hidden.

Haunted Cemeteries

Cemeteries are the depositories for the deceased, a place where loved ones are interred and visited by the living who mourn their memories, kneeling in front of etched stones. Throughout Westmoreland County, it seems as if, on occasion, the dead are the ones who visit the living. We have visited the graves of Barr Fort back in Chapter One, but now we will explore the graveyards of the towns scattered throughout the region. Like most places around here, these graveyards are indeed historical, marking the lives and events of those who have gone before us. So let us now visit a few of these cemeteries and discover what ghosts still wander these lonesome places.

Fort Barr Cemetery

In chapter one, we investigated the ghosts that still haunt the vicinity of the sites of the Barr and Wallace forts. But an interesting feature of the location of the Barr Fort is that a cemetery exists of those defenders of this fortification. A white fence surrounds the graves, an American flag waving proudly over the headstones. But indeed, this cemetery also has ghostly apparitions attached to it.

Many witnesses still report paranormal phenomena happening around the Fort Barr cemetery area. Teenagers used to do a lot of camping in this secluded area. Many claim to have heard the startled cries of horses in the dead of night, witnesses even reporting the spectral sounds of guns firing in a quick succession of three rounds, and the frenzied yelling of unseen figures. One witness said he was scared to death and refused to unzip the tent until morning when all the ghostly commotion had ceased with the rising of the sun.

There are also the reports of electric voice phenomena, or EVPs, recording the faint yet comprehendible voices of a man who answered to Major James Wilson, a hero of the Barr Fort attack. "He hummed Yankee Doodle," claimed one paranormal researcher, which eerily enough, is a song contemporaneous with the time in which Wilson lived.

Is this conclusive evidence that ghosts still prowl these grounds? While it does not substantiate the existence of life beyond the grave, all these residual impressions at the very least imply an impression of an historical period situated in a specific area due to traumatic events. This trauma is also witnessed in another location, the site of a fort that stood as protection against the bitter onslaught of Colonial warfare.

Fort Barr Ghost - entity or urban legend?

FORT PALMER CEMETERY

Just a short distance from the golf course, where the Fort once stood, the town of Fort Palmer has a small cemetery reportedly haunted by several spirits. As was reported in chapter one, this region had a great deal of hostility between the settlers and the Indians. This is illustrated by the reported sightings of red colored orbs moving throughout the trees that flank the Fort Palmer Cemetery. In the field of paranormal research, many orbs of varying hues of red have been reported in conjunction with Native American hauntings. One several occasions, ghostly Indians have even been seen moving through the trees, attesting to the likelihood that the reported orbs are indeed the spiritual energies of Indians who had been killed in this area.

Fort Palmer Cemetery Entrance.

One ghost said to inhabit this cemetery is the phantom of George Hill, a reverend who served the congregation at the Fairfield Presbyterian Church, one of the oldest churches in the Ligonier Valley. This church dates back at least to October 7, 1786. This old church remained standing until 1867. The church had no regular pastor until a certain Rev. George Hill was sent there in 1792 as its first pastor. He was then a young man, having preached but a few months prior to his ordained appointment at Fairfield. The young minister soon discovered the rigors of being a minister in the frontier towns of Westmoreland County. He had to divide his time between three different churches that were miles apart. Rev. Hill was a very remarkable man, both intellectually and physically, but the severe work which he did, and the long rides in cold weather told upon him, and near the close of his life his constitution became a wreck. He died June 7, 1822.

To this day, a man dressed in black, wearing a spilt-back riding frock, has been seen hurrying through the cemetery in which he is interred, his apparition apparently trying to break the habit of hurrying between appointments.

Fort Palmer Slab Grave.

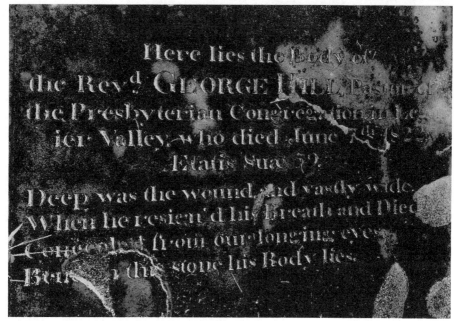

Etching from slab grave:

Here lies the Body of
the Revd GEORGE HILL Pastor of
the Presbyterian Congregation Ligon
ier Valley who died June 7, 1822
Ætatis Suae 52 [*Latin for "In the Year of Age"*]
Deep was the wound and vastly wide
When he resign'd his Breath and Died
Concealed from our longing eyes
Beneath this stone his Body lies.

OLD SALEM CHURCH CEMETERY

Sitting atop a steep hill known colloquially as Sugar Foot Hill, Old Salem Church glowers over the verdant landscape sprawled out before it. Its ancient sandstone markers, some nearly illegible with the passage of time, stand as silent testaments to lives that carved out a little space in this "howling wilderness" that once was Westmoreland County.

Old Salem Cemetery as seen today.

Founded in 1786 in Derry Township, Salem Presbyterian Church was its original name. At this time there was no meeting house; a simply tent was utilized as the place of worship. Later, the congregation built a log structure with a fireplace and called it a session house, which signified that it was used for small meetings.

The Chapel from outside - ghostly figures are sometimes seen in the reflections from the graveyard.

Four years later, in 1790, Salem Church and Unity Church, the presbyters elected a minister to serve both churches in this rural area. Reverend John McPherrin was called to be the minister to the people of these churches. After all, Rev. McPherrin was regarded as a Godly man and one of the best ministers in the area. He was installed on the 10th of September and preached for 13 years, which was to be quite appropriate. For as it turned out, the thirteenth year of his duty as minister was to be unlucky for Rev. McPherrin. For some unspecified reason, although it was enough to cause an internal scandal within the two churches he served, Rev. McPherrin was released from his duties. Now the Reverend's Godly complexion changed and he cursed the congregation for doing this to him!

Rev. McPherrin's curse seems to have backfired, however. For in death, the cemetery in the yard of the church that banished him seems to be his ghostly cell. His ghost has been seen pacing the grounds, past the old weathered slate stones, as if he is simply doing time for a crime committed many years ago.

Old Salem Headstone with Finger Pointing to Heaven.

Hankey Church Road Cemetery

In Murrysville, the Hankey Church Road Cemetery is reputed to be the haunt of a lynched minister. Those visiting this cemetery have indeed reported many of strange encounters and occurrences through the years. Some witnesses have reported the dizzying sensation of being weightless, while others have reported uncharacteristic numbness throughout their body.

It has been said that the headstones and trees in this cemetery have been seen glowing with an unexplained luminescence, and cloud-like apparitions have been witnessed floating though the cemetery on various occasions as well. One particular gravesite has a gravestone carved into the shape of a tree trunk; this area, for whatever reason, is believed to be at the center of the paranormal activity that haunts the cemetery. Some believe the minister who haunts this cemetery was hanged. Does this gravestone, fashioned like a tree, with the name Elmer E etched into it, refer to the dead minister? Or is this minister simply an urban legend? Do urban legends form as ghostly fog and chase you through the gravestones in cemeteries?

During the balmy summer months, some people report a drop in temperature so drastic that it snow falls within the cemetery! So much for urban legends. But something far more sinister seems to be at play in this place as well.

Demonic possessions have been reported in this cemetery, an apparent outpouring of the evil from the murder of the minister. It has been said that if the cemetery's gates are closed, the spirits are confined to the graveyard, but if they're open, the ghosts are free to wander. We can only hope the gates are closed.

The Old Brush Creek Cemetery

Ardara is a speck of a town that still holds remnants of the coke mines that formerly fueled its existence. Outside of this town is the graveyard known as Leger Road Cemetery. This place is also known as Old Bush Creek Cemetery, and it has a great deal of history behind its rusty and decaying fence. The exact date this cemetery was formed is uncertain, but it was certainly before the establishment of the Brush Creek Presbyterian Church, which was founded in 1784. Sometime after 1840 but before 1850, the church was closed down. Since then it has been an inactive cemetery. Well, inactive for the living, that is!

Leger Road leading up to the cemetery is in shambles, pockmarked with potholes and devoid of houses nearly a half a mile before entering the cemetery. Some people have reported being followed by shadow figures, both while approaching the cemetery and leaving it. Strange noises, moans, and even occasional bestial howls, have been heard following cars along this road. Strange black animal shapes, twisted and grotesque, have been seen following closely behind cars. These entities and the accompanying noises instantly provoke feelings of dread to all those who are witnesses to them, and many adventurous ghost hunters abandon their expedition due to the experiences they witnessed along the road. But the hauntings do indeed continue within the cemetery itself.

Many orbs and wispy images have been photographed within the confines of this cemetery. Some mediums sense the Old Brush Creek Cemetery is haunted by the spirits of Choctaw Indians who were attacked by English settlers on this site during the French and Indian War. In actuality, ghostly Indians have been seen within the gate of the cemetery, shadowy figures, tall and stately, moving almost ceremonially in this place.

The overwhelming feeling within this cemetery is one of paranoia. Many witnesses have reported the undeniably sensation of being watched as they drove up Leger Road and being followed closely while within the cemetery itself. The one prominent ghostly presence is of a shadowy entity standing behind a tree that grows in the middle of the cemetery. Some people have reported this figure leaning against the tree, watching them intently, as they got out of their car in the parking lot.

There are many graves of very young children buried in this cemetery. These young energies produce restless spirits. Crying has been reported in the dead of night, or the sound of rocks being thrown has been heard. Occasionally small shadowy figures of translucent white have been seen wafting throughout the graveyard.

Another reported white mass has been witnessed moving across the cemetery, usually appearing when you are leaving the cemetery. Is this the protective spirit of the graveyard escorting intruders out of the domain of the dead, or perhaps, it is a spirit attempting to follow you home.

OLIVE CEMETERY

The Olive Cemetery is located in Murrysville. Ireland native Jeremiah Murry founded this town. He immigrated to Pennsylvania in 1781, acquiring land near Turtle Creek where he built a cabin and gristmill. Murry established the town of Murrysville in 1820, no more than a year after the Northern Turnpike was constructed. He originally purchased several hundred acres of land, which he subdivided into streets and lots. Murry then sold the land to incoming settlers. Many of these settlers are interred at Olive Cemetery.

This graveyard is on Logan's Ferry Road, just off Holiday Park Drive, by the deserted Olive Reformed Church. The cemetery, which dates back officially to 1817, is said to be haunted by the ghost of ferry operator named Alexander Logan. His ghost is said to be cantankerous, materializing to chase away trespassers who venture into the confines of the cemetery.

BOLIVAR CEMETERY OF WEST VIEW

The Bolivar West View Cemetery sits on a hill, surrounded by trees, frequently shrouded in mist as fog rolls in off the Conemaugh River. Here lies immigrants and wealthy business owners, the very young interred next to the very old. Bolivar was a microcosm of Westmoreland County towns, and the cemetery attests to this. And so do its ghosts.

The area that became known as Bolivar was established as a village by Scottish and Irish canal workers about the time of the building of the Pennsylvania Canal. After the building of the canal was in full swing, these few immigrant workers sent money to bring their families and relatives here.

These settlers to this still unnamed area eventually held a meeting in one of their log cabins to decide a name for anonymous town. These immigrants decided it should be named Washington in honor of their new country's heroic General, George Washington. They wanted this name because they knew of his feats in bringing freedom and liberty to these shores. The Post Office Department, however, suggested to them that they should think of another name since Washington was the name of many towns, cities, and villages. These immigrants also knew of Simon Bolivar, the great liberator of South America, who was sometimes referred to as the George Washington of South America. Thus, the people of this area called the town and the post office Bolivar. This place was then incorporated as a town in 1865.

The cemetery in Bolivar, known as the West View Cemetery, is a memorial to what life was like in these hardworking towns, indicative of the way of life throughout most of Westmoreland County in the mid-19th century through the early 20th century. One ghostly gray man, seen dressed in a top hat and wearing a suit jacket with a neat ascot tied about his neck, was reported by a sensitive named Leah Dawn Madden. He was one of the many men who built a fortune from the raw materials of this region. He is seen occasionally, faintly perceived standing under the tree that shades his grave. He has even been known to tip his hat to the ladies who unknowingly wander by his haunt.

As this ghost demonstrates, many people did in fact amass riches from the commodities mined of shipped through this area. But as many men prospered, ten times that many labored under the ground in mines or worked the railroad. For the laborers, earning a living wage often cost them their lives. In 1907, several industrial disasters hit Bolivar. There were two fatal railway accidents in this year. The first, in October of 1907, involved a train accident.

Angel statues pray for the departed in the West View Cemetery.

As has been witnessed throughout Westmoreland County, ghostly miners have been seen walking through the grave markers in this secluded cemetery outside of Bolivar. They wear the traditional miner gear, some still covered in the dust of the mine that took their life. These ghosts are spectral testaments to life underground and to death that came far too often for the many who eked a living underground.

But the victims of the mines and labor tragedies are not the only ones interred in this cemetery. Because Bolivar was situated on the rail-line, the trains unfortunately brought more than passengers and goods. Modern transportation brought with it the flu. The flu pandemic during the early 20th century has been described as "the greatest medical holocaust in history." Indeed, by some accounts, this flu outbreak may have killed more people than the Black Death claimed lives in Europe! Even isolated towns like Bolivar, tucked away in the hills, could not escape its influence. Trains brought the infection into this town, and indeed throughout Westmoreland County and all of Pennsylvania. The flu was the primary infection, but the secondary cause of most deaths was pneumonia. Whooping cough was also prevalent as an ancillary effect of this brutal plague.

In this cemetery of West View, you can see the effects of this flu pandemic, white gravestones illustrating the grim fact that entire families were wiped out by this epidemic. In 1918, one in five American children did not live beyond their fifth birthday. One ghostly figure of a woman, shrouded in the black hues of mourning, has been seen at the edge of the forest that encircles this graveyard. She is sometimes heard audibly weeping for the loss of her children, taken from her as the epidemic swept through her town. Indeed, the cruel fact may be that she not only had to watch her children slowly succumb to this dread malady, but she, too, may have eventually died in the same outbreak that claimed her children. As no spirits of children have ever been reported in this cemetery, it seems as if they may have passed on, and the mother, inconsolable with grief, helplessly watching as her children died, one by one, simply cannot reconcile the fact that her children were taken from her so soon.

THE GHOSTS OF THE GRAVEYARD AT ST. VINCENT

On the holy grounds of this landmark just outside of Latrobe, images of the faces of long deceased monks and nuns have been seen roaming about in the cemetery. Sometimes these religious figures are even seen filing along with an occasional residual funeral procession!

There is also the tale of a tree stump that, legend claims, is carved into a wooden throne by the little boy whose grave is beside it. Some students at the college actually have claimed to see a small ghostly figure of a boy sitting in it.

In another part of the cemetery is a statue of the Blessed Mother. This statue of Mary is said to weep tears of blood when someone with genuine sorrow prays to her, in sympathy of that person's pain.

There is yet another haunted religious statue in the cemetery of St. Vincent. In the middle of the graveyard is a Pieta statue of Mary holding the lifeless body of her son, Jesus, after he has been taken down from the cross. Witnesses have attested that if you sit on a bench in front of this Pieta long enough, the carved figure of Mary will raise her head and look at you.

Besides these phantom clerics and nuns and spirited statuary, other more traditional specters float throughout this cemetery. It is regularly reported that foggy entities spotted in the graveyard by security guards vanish without a trace, at first seen as full-bodied apparitions then simply dissipating before their very eyes!

THE SISTER'S CEMETERY AT SETON HILL UNIVERSITY

Outside of Greensburg, at the cemetery on the campus of Seton Hill, a woman reported witnessing a ghostly figure cross through the cemetery. The woman stopped her car to allow this "person" the right of way to cross the road in front of Brownlee Hall, but when the driver motioned the figure across, she disappeared into a fog. This purported female phantom could be the spirit of any of the cemetery's interred, of whom 785 are sisters.

The graveyard was planned and laid out in 1889 when the Seton Hill Motherhouse was completed. It's the final resting place of the Seton Hill Sisters of Charity, the founders of the university, all the past presidents, and several other notable priests, laymen, and laywomen. A little boy is one spook, playing with a ball and occasionally running like someone is chasing him, screaming all the while. Another tale is of a woman who stops traffic on the road so she can cross (or hitch a ride), but when the driver brakes and looks for her, she has already disappeared into the fog. Also reported spotted in the college graveyard are the spirits of sisters, gone and buried, who once lived at Seton Hill, along with some EVPs. One story regarding demonic grave circles can be discounted, though. The original layout of the sisters' burial plots was circular, but that proved to be too space consuming, and was replaced by the traditional rows of graves.

Sister's Cemetery overlooking the campus.

Seton Hill Cemetery Gates.

However, it is not the ghost of a religious woman that is most often reported in this graveyard. Indeed, the haunt in this cemetery most often reported by students is the recurring ghost of a little boy. He has appeared on numerous occasions, sometimes in full daylight, scampering among the headstones or playing hide and seek behind the trees. There is, in fact, no child buried in this cemetery, but some claim it is the ghost of a child of a nun who kept her condition and subsequent birth a secret before sending the child away for adoption. If this is indeed the circumstances, is it possible the child may return to the place of his birth, seeking out his birthmother?

There is one other ghost reported wandering about this cemetery. It is the ghost of a man, tall and stately dressed, moving purposefully through the cemetery before disappearing as he nears the gate that surrounds the graveyard. The cemetery does, in fact, have men buried in it. Three of the male burials, that of a Monsignor William Granger Ryan, Rev. Daniel R. Sullivan, and Rev. J.A. Reeves, were former presidents of Seton Hill College. Another reverend, Rev. N. Albanese, albeit not a president, was still very close to the sisters and was thus buried in Seton Hill's cemetery. The only two laymen buried there were a carpenter and a watchman, both who lived on the property. It seems one of these men are the residual energies left over from a life focused so acutely on their beloved Seton Hill University.

AVONMORE CEMETERY

The town of Avonmore itself is the mere ghost of the town it once was when coal was king and the community was prosperous. With the economy gone the way of the mines, now only about 350 people live in this declining village. Indeed, it may well be that more ghosts inhabit this town than the living!

The spirits of various elderly individuals have been seen among the walking among the stones of the abandoned graveyard, forming a procession out of the cemetery and vanishing in a field adjacent to where their bodies are buried. The field by the graveyard, it is alleged, is the location of the intended site of a church that was never built because of a disagreement among the congregation. The spirits of the cemetery apparently were displeased with this decision not to build the church at the site, their ghosts seen wandering about and processing to the where this church was supposed to stand. Maybe, just maybe, this church does exist on a different plane of existence and the ghosts are lining up and filing in to attend church services.

THE CEMETERY OF LIVERMORE

Livermore is such a haunted ghost town that it had to have its own chapter devoted to the otherworldly goings on encountered in this vicinity of Westmoreland County. Researchers have videotaped orbs moving throughout the cemetery, and EVPs have recorded ghostly conversations. But full-bodied apparitions have been reported at this little graveyard that overlooks the Conemaugh River–the same river that caused the demise of the town to which this cemetery once belonged. Here are but a few of the sightings reported from this cemetery.

The ghost house, so often seen in the area of the former town, has been witnessed around this hilltop resting place numerous times and, like a mirage, simply vanishes when approached. Sometimes, it has been seen shimmering among the stones, other times it has been witnessed in the adjoining cornfield. Other times it has been reported in the forest like a ghostly witch's habitation told in fairytales. But more than a phantom house haunts the cemetery of Livermore.

Children that had succumbed to the flu epidemic still play around the gravestones that mark the burial spot of their corporeal bodies. They appear to have no idea that they are no longer alive, as they have been seen gaily gallivanting among the headstones, sometimes even interacting with other young children who visit the graveyard. It seems as if they are content in this place, making up for lost time that was taken from them by death's icy embrace.

From an historical perspective, one of the more noteworthy ghosts is that of a certain private from Company C of the US Cavalry. John B. McGuire, a resident of this area, returned to Westmoreland County after his service in the Indian Wars. You see, Pvt. McGuire served under General George Armstrong Custard at the ill-fated Battle of Little Bighorn. Not everyone was massacred in this attack, and McGuire and several other men hid out in scrub brush as the attack raged around them. They were court-marshaled and returned from service deemed as cowards. But on several occasions, the ghost of McGuire has been seen racing through the cemetery, seemingly pursued by unseen forces. In one sighting, the private was seen in full military regalia astride a phantom horse! His energy was apparently imprinted where his body lies and images of his tumultuous service flicker from time to time in a phantasmal series of instances from the war.

Grave marker at Livermore Cemetery.

A black hunched figure has been seen roaming through the fog that often engulfs the Livermore cemetery. Immediately those who witness this vacuous specter assume it is the ghost of the witch which legend maintains cursed this area nearly two hundred years ago. Although a face is never seen, witnesses unanimously claim that it is a female spirit and she is better left alone. This cemetery has been used for occultic practices for nearly four decades. Could this be a spirit summoned through the Ouija board on some night under a full moon? Or is this the apparition of someone that was indeed executed for presumed demonic collaboration? One psychic stated that this ghost, although appearing to be in the general shape of a human, never was human. This black figure, it is said, is a hellish spirit that prowls about seeking those who ignore the "No Trespassing" sign on the fence that bars the road from visitors.

It may be best to heed the sign and not intrude on this domain of the dead.

AFTER THOUGHTS...

So, for now, our investigation into the haunted happenings of Westmoreland County is at an end. We didn't run out of stories; we ran out of the places to put them! We followed a rather rigid format, structured on the colonialization, transportation, industry, learning, worship, and entertainment in this County. Next time we will look at what we didn't cover here.

I'm proud to call this region my home. It is in my blood and it flows into the words I put on the page. Without this land and its people, I would not be the person I am today.

The lives I have written about had meaning. They made an impact in the era in which they lived. For good or bad, these stories are about visceral people that made this area their home. They are our kin, our ancestors of this human experience. I hope you enjoyed encountering these ghosts as much as I enjoyed conjuring them. The history they made helped create the America we know today. And that is something we should be proud of.

BIBLIOGRAPHY

Albert, George Dallas. Forts of Western Pennsylvania. Harrisburg, 1916

Bicentennial History Commission. 200 Years of History. New Alexandria Westmoreland County PA. 1976

Boucher, John N. History of Westmoreland County, Pa. New York: The Lewis Publishing Company, 1906.

Braden, Edward. Derry Area Historical Sketches. 1934

Neman, John A. Coal Company Store Prices Questioned: A Case Study of the Union Supply Company, 1905-1906.

Hassler, Edgar Wakefield Old Westmoreland: A History of Western Pennsylvania During the Revolution. Pittsburgh: J. R. Weldin and Company, 1900.

Matrya, Mickey Remembrance of Bairdstown. 1999

Myers, Paul. Westmoreland County in the American Revolution. Closson Press, 1988.

Olsen, Merle Area Forts. 2001

Thomas, Eleanor Community Express

www.incommunitymagazine.com/historic-landmarks-restored

Pittsburgh Post Gazette "Here: In Latrobe." January 18, 2004.

Pittsburgh Tribune Review "G-E-T O-U-T Chases UPG Students" October 31, 2008.

Sources cited are from Haunted Seton Hill and the Pittsburgh Tribune Review "Horror Film Begins Production at 'Creepy' Seton Hill," December 7, 2007.

PHOTO CREDITS

Westmoreland County, PA: U.S. Census Bureau, 2000. Public Domain. Modified Jan. 2016 <http://www2.census.gov/geo/maps/general_ref/cousub_outline/cen2k_pgsz/pa_cosub.pdf>

Derry Station, PA Aerial View: Fowler & Moyer, 1900. Lib. of Cong. Public Domain. Web. 27 Jan. 2016. <http://hdl.loc.gov/loc.gmd/g3824d.pm007611>.

Ligonier, PA Aerial View: Fowler & Moyer, 1900. Lib. of Cong. Public Domain. Web. 27 Jan. 2016. <http://hdl.loc.gov/loc.gmd/g3824l.pm007970>.

Fort Ligonier, PA: Jeff Kubina, 2007. cc-by-sa-2.0. Retr. 27 Jan. 2016 <http://flickr.com/photos/95118988@N00/498303484>

Fort Ligonier Soldier Barracks and Quartermaster Store, Ligonier PA

Fort Ligonier Barracks, 2012: Wilson44691, 2012. cc-by-sa-3.0. Retr. 27 Jan. 2016 <https://commons.wikimedia.org/wiki/File:Fort_Ligonier_Barracks_060512.JPG>

Chief Pontiac in 1763 taking up the war hatchet in the French and Indian War. Color engraving from the 19th century.

Pontiac in 1763: Unknown, 19th century. Public Domain. Modified. 27 Jan 2016 <https://commons.wikimedia.org/wiki/File:Pontiac_in_1763.jpg>

Sketch from Clarence M. Busch's report to the PA historical commission in 1896 to document the history of frontier forts in Western PA Sketch of Bouquet's Engagements, 1763: Busch, Clarence M, 1896. REPORT OF THE COMMISSION TO LOCATE THE SITE OF THE FRONTIER FORTS OF PENNSYLVANIA. VOLUME TWO. Public Domain. Courtesy of Westmoreland Historical Society. Retr. 27. Jan 2016 <http://www.usgwarchives.net/pa/1pa/1picts/frontierforts/ff36.html>

Bushy Run Battlefield with 250th Anniversary Memorial

Bushy Run Memorial, 2013: Ronald L. Murphy, Jr. cc-by-sa-3.0. Modified 27 Jan. 2016

Bushy Run Battlefield Historical Marker

Bushy Run Battlefield Marker, 2013: Ronald L. Murphy, Jr., 2013. Modified 27 Jan. 2016

John Peebles Memorial Plaque. Veteran of the Battle of Bushy Run: Rosser1954, 2013. cc-by-sa-3.0. Modified 26 Jan. 2016. <https://commons.wikimedia.org/wiki/File:John_Peebles,_memorial_plaque,_Irvine.JPG>

Severe weathering on plaque - photo negative for legibility

Text: Here Rests the Mortal Part of John Peebles. Late Capt'n of Grenadiers 42nd Regiment. Subsquently Major Commandant of the Irvine Volunteers. Born 11th Sept. 1739. Died 7th Dec. 1823. (Aged Eighty Four Years) For Upwards of Forty Years He Served His King and Country with Fidelity and was Severely Wounded at the Battle of Bushy Run in the Warfare (North American Indians in 1763)

Hanna's Town in 1770s: Homer F. Blair, 1941. Retrieved 26. Jan. 2016. Courtesy of Latrobe Bulletin.

Reconstruction of Hanna's Tavern (the original courthouse and jail)

Old Hanna's Town Historic Site, Reconstruction: Roy Klotz, 2013. cc by-sa 3.0. Modified 27 Jan. 2016. <https://en.wikipedia.org/wiki/Site_of_Old_Hannastown#/media/File:SITE_OF_OLD_HANNASTOWN,_WESTMORELAND_COUNTY,_PA.jpg>

Hanna's Town Historical Plaque, 2013: Ronald L. Murphy, Jr. cc-by-sa-3.0. Modified 28 Jan. 2016. Ronald L. Murphy, Jr., 2015. cc-by-sa-3.0.

Historic Hannastown Sign: Ronald L. Murphy, Jr., 2015.

Historic Hannastown Old Fort Walls: Ronald L. Murphy, Jr., 2015.

Fort Palmer Cemetery: Ronald L. Murphy, Jr., 2015.

Trail Near Cokeville: Ronald L. Murphy, Jr., 2015.

Fort Palmer Coke Works Ruins of Belgian Ovens: coalandcoke.blogspot.com, 2013. <http://coalandcoke.blogspot.com/search/label/Fort%20Palmer%20Coke%20Works>

Old Retaining Wall from the Cokeville canal: coalandcoke.blogspot.com, 2013. <http://coalandcoke.blogspot.com/search/label/Cokeville%20PA>

Overgrown railroad bridge abutment in near Cokeville: coalandcoke.blogspot.com, 2013. <http://coalandcoke.blogspot.com/search/label/Cokeville%20PA>

Traditional Gadsden Flag "Don't Tread on Me": Christopher Gadsden, 1775. Public Domain. <https://en.wikipedia.org/wiki/Gadsden_flag#/media/File:Gadsden_flag.svg>

Standard of the 1st Battalion Westmoreland County PA aka "Proctor's Flag." Created as a direct result of Hanna's Town Resolves. Only surviving colonial era "rattlesnake design" flag. Gold paint on red cloth: unknown designer from Hanna's Town, 1775. Public Domain.

Remnants of the original Braddock's Road: Wilson44691, 2014. cc0 (released into public domain). <https://en.wikipedia.org/wiki/Braddock_Road_%28Braddock_expedition%29#/media/File:Braddock_Road_Fort_Necessity_PA.jpg>

Historical Marker of Old Forbes Road near Ligonier, 1758:

Map of Forbes' Road and Braddock's Road: Courtesy Derry Area Historical Society.

Marker for Forbes' Road on the Laurel Highlands Hiking Trail:

The Compass Inn, Laughlintown, PA: Canadian2006, 2007. cc-by-sa-3.0. <https://en.wikipedia.org/wiki/Compass_Inn#/media/File:Compass_Inn_Pennsylvania.jpg>

The Washington Furnace Inn: photographer unknown, 1930s.

R&R Station Restaurant: Ronald L. Murphy, Jr., 2015.

Congruity Stagecoach Inn:

Coal Barge Pulled up Canal by Mules, 1904: Frank Hill, 1904. Lib. of Cong. Public Domain. <http://hdl.loc.gov/loc.pnp/cph.3b15770>

Delaware & Hudson Co. Canal Coal Pocket, Wayne, PA: C P (photographer initials only), exact year unknown. Lib. of Cong. Public Domain. <http://www.loc.gov/pictures/item/pa1626.photos.141918p>

Miner and mule at American Radiator Mine, Mount Pleasant, Westmoreland County, Pennsylvania: Carl Mydans, 1936. Lib. of Cong. Public Domain. <http://hdl.loc.gov/loc.pnp/fsa.8a00917>

Miners at American Radiator Mine, Mount Pleasant, Westmoreland County, Pennsylvania: Carl Mydans, 1936. Lib. of Cong. Public Domain. <http://hdl.loc.gov/loc.pnp/fsa.8a00947>

The Compass Inn, Laughlintown, PA: Ronald L. Murphy, Jr., 2015.

Irish Railroad Workers, B&O Railroad: photographer unknown, 1850-59. Public Domain. Courtesy of B&O Railroad Museum.

Surveying the wreckage of the 1912 Ligonier Valley Railroad Accident: photographer unknown, 1912. Public Domain.

Greensburg PA Railroad Station: Ronald L. Murphy, Jr., 2015.

Latrobe PA Railroad Station: Ronald L. Murphy, Jr., 2015.

Derry Quarry, Overturned Cars: Public Domain. Courtesy Derry Area Historical Society.

Derry Quarry, Track Repairs following Accident: Public Domain. Courtesy Derry Area Historical Society.

Derry Quarry, Car on Tracks Lowered Down Hill on Cable: Public Domain. Courtesy Derry Area Historical Society.

Derry Quarry, Rail Shed Destroyed following Accident: Public Domain. Courtesy Derry Area Historical Society.

Derry Quarry, early photograph: Public Domain. Courtesy Derry Area Historical Society.

Westmoreland Glass Company Furnace 1: Jet Lowe, 1950s?. Lib. of Cong. Public Domain. <http://hdl.loc.gov/loc.pnp/hhh.pa3038/photos.358262p>

Westmoreland Glass Company, Post Fire, 2013.

Coal Miners Descending into Hazleton Mine: 1905. Lib. of Cong. Public Domain. <http://hdl.loc.gov/loc.pnp/cph.3b04484>

Miner Trapped in Cave in: c. 1909-1930. Lib. of Cong. Public Domain. <http://hdl.loc.gov/loc.pnp/cph.3b24667>

PA Miners prep for dynomite blasting: Sheldon Dick, 1938. Lib. of Cong. Public Domain. <http://hdl.loc.gov/loc.pnp/fsa.8c28708>

Greensburg Police Chief Joseph Boomer from 1888-1920s: c. 1900. Public Domain. Courtesy Greensburg Police Department.

Members of Black Hand Arrested in Fairmont, WV: c. 1903-1910. Lib. of Cong. Public Domain. <http://hdl.loc.gov/loc.pnp/ggbain.03246>

Black Hand Blackmail Symbols: c. 1904. Public Domain.

Aeriel View of Monessen, Pittsburgh Steel Company Blast Furnace & Coke Plant: Jet Lowe, date unknown. Lib. of Cong. Public Domain. <http://hdl.loc.gov/loc.pnp/hhh.pa2744/photos.356929p>

Lehigh Specialty Melting Co.: Ronald L. Murphy, Jr., 2015.

Mount Pleasant Aeriel Drawing: Fowler & Moyer, 1900. Lib. of Cong. Public Domain. <http://hdl.loc.gov/loc.gmd/g3824m.pm008102>

Packsaddle Gap: 1891. Photographer Unknown. Public Domain.

Packsaddle Gap from the water: Ronald L. Murphy, Jr., 2015.

St. Vincent College & Basilica: Ronald L. Murphy, Jr., 2015.

Seton Hill Sign & Gravestones: Ronald L. Murphy, Jr., 2015.

Seton Hill Graveyard Gates: Ronald L. Murphy, Jr., 2015.

Seton Hill Main Entrance with Elizabeth Ann Seton Statue: Irteagle102704, 2007. Released to Public Domain. <https://commons.wikimedia.org/wiki/File:SHU_front.jpg>

Lynch Hall at University of Pitt-Greensburg: Michael G. White, 2008. cc-by-sa-3.0.   <https://en.wikipedia.org/wiki/University_of_Pittsburgh_at_Greensburg#/media/File:LynchHall.jpg>

Seton Hill St. Joseph's Chapel Interior: Kayla Sawyer, 2009. cc-by-sa-2.0.

St. Martin's Church in Derry: Ronald L. Murphy, Jr., 2015.

Indiana Gazette Headline of Derry Copter Crash: Indiana Gazette, 1978.

St. Joseph's Roman Catholic Church: Ronald L. Murphy, Jr., 2015.

Livermore Station in 1908, Pennsylvania Railroad Line: 1908. Public Domain.

Headline from Minneapolis Daily Globe, Johnstown Flood: 1889. Lib. of Cong. Public Domain. <http://www.loc.gov/rr/news/topics/johnstown.html#links>

Johnstown Flood Damage: Histed, 1889. Lib. of. Cong. Public Domain. <http://hdl.loc.gov/loc.pnp/ppmsca.17548>

Scottdale, PA: 1910. Public Domain. Courtesy Brown Street Clock Registry.

Geyer Performing Arts Center, Scottdale: 2012. Courtesy Geyer Performing Arts Center.

Casino Theater, Vandergrift, PA: photographer unknown. Courtesy Casino Theater/Anthony Ferrente.

Palace Theatre, Greensburg, PA: Ronald L. Murphy, Jr., 2015.

Gem Theatre Ticket, Derry, PA: Courtesy Derry Area Historical Society.

Historic Gem Theatre Facade, Derry, PA: Courtesy Derry Area Historical Society.

Greensburg, PA County Courthouse: Ronald L. Murphy, Jr., 2015.

Evans Execution, Register of Pennsylvania: Samuel Hazard, 1830. Public Domain.

Torrance State Hospital Outbuilding: Ronald L. Murphy, Jr., 2015.

Torrance State Hospital Panorama: Ronald L. Murphy, Jr., 2015.

Torrance State Hospital Unused Wing: Ronald L. Murphy, Jr., 2015.

Barr Fort Ghost, Urban Legend?: photographer unknown.

Fort Palmer Slab Grave (Etching for Inscription): Ronald L. Murphy, Jr., 2015.

Fort Palmer Slab Grave: Ronald L. Murphy, Jr., 2015.

Old Salem Window: Ronald L. Murphy, Jr., 2015.

Old Salem Window 2: Ronald L. Murphy, Jr., 2015.

Old Salem Headstone with Finger Pointing to Heaven: Ronald L. Murphy, Jr., 2015.

Old Salem Ruined Graves: Ronald L. Murphy, Jr., 2015.

Old Salem Cemetery: Ronald L. Murphy, Jr., 2015.

Bolivar Angel Statue: Ronald L. Murphy, Jr., 2015.

Livermore - McGuire Headstone: Ronald L. Murphy, Jr., 2015.

Derry Ridge Quarry Accident: WTAE 4 News Coverage, 2015.

Derry Round House: Public Domain.

Cokeville Baseball Team: 1893. Public Domain.

Cokeville, Walkinshaw Building and Milliron Store: 1890s. Public Domain.

Cokeville, USGS Map: 1902. Public Domain.